Treasures From The Dust

Also by
Azriel Eisenberg and Dov Peretz Elkins

WORLDS LOST AND FOUND
Discoveries in Biblical Archeology

Treasures From The Dust

BY AZRIEL EISENBERG AND DOV PERETZ ELKINS

ILLUSTRATED BY MICHAEL HOPKINS

ABELARD-SCHUMAN   New York ● London

Dedicated to our little treasures:
Hillel, Jonathan and Shira Elkins
Debbie, Naomi and Daniel Eisenberg

ACKNOWLEDGMENTS

The authors would like to thank several gracious scholars who gave of their valuable time to read parts of the manuscript, and made helpful suggestions. Final responsibility, of course, lies with the authors themselves. We offer sincere thanks to Professors David N. Freedman, James B. Pritchard, Nahum M. Sarna, Jacob Neusner, Shalom M. Paul, Bezalel Porten, Shlomo Baltar, and Alan B. Lettofsky.

Gratitude is also extended to Mr. and Mrs. Preston Epstein, who read the proofs, and to Bruce Horovitz and Edith Gendzier, who read the proofs and compiled the index.

Published on the same day in Canada
by Longman Canada Limited

NEW YORK	LONDON
Abelard-Schuman	Abelard-Schuman
Limited	Limited
257 Park Ave. S.	158 Buckingham Palace Road SW1
10010	24 Market Square, Aylesbury

An Intext Publisher

Printed in the United States of America

First published in Great Britain in 1973.

Library of Congress Cataloging in Publication Data
Eisenberg, Azriel Louis, 1903-
    Treasures from the dust.
    SUMMARY: Describes the technical aspects of several important archaeological digs in the Middle East and what their discoveries have revealed about ancient civilizations.
    Bibliography: p.
    1. Near East—Antiquities. 2. Bible—Antiquities. [1. Bible—Antiquities. 2. Near East—Antiquities. 3. Archaeology] I. Elkins, Dov Peretz, joint author. II. Hopkins, Michael, illus. III. Title.
DS56.E47   913.9   78-156583
ISBN 0-200-71827-4

CONTENTS

	Introduction..	vii
	List of Illustrations......................................	ix
Chapter 1	THE CODE OF HAMMURABI: The Golden Age of Babylon...	1
2	FROM PICTURES TO SYMBOLS, TO WEDGE SHAPES, TO WRITING: The Triumph of the Alphabet........................	15
3	THE FAT OLD KING WHO CONQUERED ISRAEL: The Story of the Merneptah Stele..................................	26
4	HAZOR, THE HEAD OF ALL THOSE KINGDOMS: A Dig That Will Take Eight Hundred Years..................................	34
5	AN ARCHEOLOGIST GOES TO COURT: Excavations of King Saul's Palace at Gibeah..................................	41
6	THE ANCIENT WEIGHT THAT SOLVED A PUZZLE: The Story of How a Biblical Verse Came to Life..................	49
7	THE BLACK OBELISK OF SHALMANESER III: A Non-Biblical View of a Biblical Event..................................	60
8	THE CLUE FROM THE SUN: How the Word "Hamman" Came Back to Life..	67
9	THE VAIN PRIME MINISTER: The Rediscovery of the Shebna Tomb...	75
10	WHO WAS THE LAST KING OF JUDAH?: The Story of the Jehoiachin Tablets...	85
11	FROM THE KING OF PERSIA TO THE SHAH OF IRAN: The Story of the Cyrus Cylinder..................................	95

Chapter 12   THE MYSTIFYING DURA SYNAGOGUE MURALS: "Images"
in the Synagogue.. 104

13   THE SAMARITANS AND THE DALIYEH PAPYRI: Light on a
2700 Year Old Jewish Sect 114

14   PRICELESS TREASURES UNDER FIRE: The Dead Sea
Scrolls During the Six Day War.................................... 125

15   THE CHOCOLATE-COVERED DEAD SEA SCROLL: The
Story of Yigael Yadin and the Temple Scroll 134

Bibliography... 143

Index... 147

INTRODUCTION

Treasures from the Dust rounds out a group of forty-five stories told by the authors in four volumes. Beginning with *The Great Discovery* (a book about the Dead Sea Scrolls discovered in 1947), these stories tell about ancient peoples, buried civilizations, and cities of the Bible, as well as of the kings and prophets who moulded Judaism and Christianity. They include chapters on the new science of underwater archeology, and give an insight into the development of the alphabet and the decipherment of forgotten languages. The books also shed light on the great help archeology has been in the new scientific translations of the Bible which have been published recently by Jewish, Catholic and Protestant groups.

In the telling of these stories the reader is introduced to leading archeologists such as Henry Breasted and Nelson Glueck, Flinders Petrie and Yigael Yadin, George Smith and Eliezer Sukenik, and many others who have uncovered treasures from the dust of ages and rediscovered lost worlds.

In the present volume the story of the most important ancient social document discovered thus far, the Code of Hammurabi, is narrated. This book also describes a dig that may take eight hundred years to complete; a sect that broke away from the Jews 2700 years ago and is at long last becoming united with their brethren; and how three very old pieces of bronze and stone helped to solve a hopelessly obscure verse in the Book of Samuel. Other stories relate why the State of Israel celebrated the twenty-fifth hundred anniversary of an ancient Persian emperor; which scrolls and documents have been recently discovered in the arid Judean caves; and what happened to the precious Dead Sea Scrolls during the Six Day War in June, 1967. These are but a few of the intriguing problems touched on in the pages that follow.

Hundreds of young people from all over the world are busy digging up the past during their summer vacations in Israel and the storied lands of the Middle East. When peace and security are restored to these troubled countries, will you join the adventurous groups of archeologists who dig the ancient mounds, sift the desert sands, wash the broken potsherds and with luck come upon finds that make history? This is the aspiration the authors have tried to instill in you. If you don't become an active digger, we hope you will at least enjoy being an armchair explorer.

Azriel Eisenberg
Dov Peretz Elkins

LIST OF ILLUSTRATIONS

Shamash receiving homage from Hammurabi, Stele of Hammurabi.................. 6
The Fertile Crescent... 19
Egyptian hieroglyph
   Gimel-camel, the third letter of the Hebrew alphabet
   Ugaritic cuneiform... 24
Sir Flinders Petrie and the Merneptah Stele
   Egyptian God Amon presenting a sword to Pharaoh Merneptah 31
Yigael Yadin with his finds at Hazor... 37
David playing the harp for King Saul... 47
Shahib picking up a metal object
   The word "Pim" and a "Pim" weight 50
Austen Henry Layard drawing at the site of Khorsabad
   The Black Obelisk of Shalmaneser III 62
Wood and Dawkins and their puzzling find.. 69
Ancient Hebrew letters above the tomb of Shebna................................... 77
Jews in captivity in Babylonia 90
The tomb of King Cyrus 96
Terra-cotta cylinder of King Cyrus 101
The mystifying murals in the synagogue at Dura.................................... 107
A Samaritan at prayer
   The Scroll of Law... 123
Palestine Archeological Museum.. 128
The Temple Scroll... 136

1

THE CODE OF HAMMURABI:
The Golden Age of Babylon

When lofty Anu, king of the Anunnaki
And Enlil, lord of heaven and earth . . .
Determined for Marduk . . .
Dominion over all mankind . . .
Then did Anu and Enlil name me,
Hammurabi, the devout, god-fearing prince,
To make justice rule in the land,
To destroy the wicked and unjust,
That the strong might not oppress the weak;
To rise like Shamash over the Mesopotamian people
And to promote the well being of the people.[1]

[1] The text of this and subsequent passages from the Code of Hammurabi are quoted from *The Face of the Ancient Orient* by Sabatino Moscati, Quadrangle Books, 1960. Permission granted by Routledge & Kegan Paul Ltd.

Thus begins the famous ancient text, the Code of Hammurabi, an inscription on a shaft of black diorite that today stands in the Louvre Museum in Paris. This stele [2] was discovered in December 1901 — January 1902 by Father Jean Vincent Scheil, a member of a French archeological expedition, headed by Jacques de Morgan.

The French expedition had been exploring Babylonia, Persia and Egypt. In 1888, de Morgan began digging in the ancient Persian city of Susa, the old capital of the Kingdom of Elam. He had found inscriptions in Babylonia which said that many centuries before Christ important monuments had been carried off, as trophies of war, by Elamite kings to Susa.

Father Scheil was the Assyrian language scholar of the team. It was evident to him that the stele had been brought to Susa from Babylon as a trophy since the inscription on it had been carved by the order of the Babylonian ruler Hammurabi. The team surmised that originally it had stood in the shrine of Marduk, the chief god of Babylonia, two hundred miles to the west of Susa.

Hammurabi was sixth in line in the first Babylonian dynasty. After his dynasty, the Semitic language and people (previously called Amorites) became known as Babylonian. Various dates have been assigned to the reign of Hammurabi. Scholars once placed it as far back as 2061 to 2004 B.C. More recently, however, the dates of 1728 to 1686 B.C. have been generally accepted. The difficulty had been that the Babylonian records offered no clue, and there appeared to be no direct connection between their records and those of other ancient peoples for whom a chronology had been established. Egypt, for example, had a reliable chronology based on the rise and fall of the Nile, which corresponds almost exactly to the solar year.

[2] Stele (from the Greek word meaning "to stand" or "to set"): an upright stone slab or pillar usually bearing an inscription memorializing a person or an event.

Babylonia had a dating system all its own. Each year was assigned a descriptive "year formula," giving what was regarded as the most significant event as a point of reference. This meant that the chronology was tied to the reign of a particular monarch. The following extracts from Hammurabi's reign will suggest the problem of assigning fixed dates:

Year 1. *In which Hammurabi became king.*
Year 2. *In which he brought justice to the land.*
Year 9. *In which Hammurabi's canal was dug.*
Year 22. *In which the statue, "Hammurabi is the king of righteousness," was prepared.*
Year 35. *In which, at the behest of Anu and Enlil, he destroyed the walls round Mari and Malgia.*
Year 42. *In which he built a wall on the banks of the Euphrates.*

In the 1930's a discovery was made that helped to synchronize the Babylonian record with the date of a fairly reliable document found among the Mari tablets near Tel Hariri, Syria.[3] Syria was then a French protectorate, and a French lieutenant stationed near Tel Hariri, on the Iraqi border, noticed some Bedouins gathering large stones and carrying them away. He asked what they were doing, and was told: "We are taking them to pile on the grave of our neighbor. If we don't, the hyenas and other wild animals will dig him up at night and devour him." During their conversation, the tribesmen also told the lieutenant that they had found a large stone in the shape of a man, but without a head. At this the lieutenant pricked up his ears, knowing that his govern-

[3] "The Man Without a Head: The Story of the Mari Archives," *Worlds Lost and Found,* Azriel Eisenberg and Dov Peretz Elkins (Abelard-Schuman, New York, 1964).

ment was very much interested in archeological exploration. His report of the conversation led to the discovery of the royal city of Mari, and a vast quantity of materials which shed light on a lost civilization. Among them was a document fixing the dates of the reign of a king of Mari who had lived in the time of Hammurabi. As a result, the dating of Hammurabi's reign from 1728 to 1686 B.C. is now fairly well established.

Hammurabi was a great empire builder. His conquests included the kingdoms of Elam to the east, and Assyria to the north. To strengthen his army, Hammurabi established strict military conscription. But his greatness was not only military. He improved the irrigation system which added cultivated land to the region. He encouraged commerce by building a canal from Kish to the Persian Gulf, and established rest and watering places for caravans. He centralized the worship of the supreme deity, Marduk, in the shrine at Esagila. Although he ruled with an iron hand, Hammurabi did not ask his subjects to look upon him as a god. Rather, he established a separation between the palace and the temple or, as we would say today, between church and state.

Under the Sumerians before Hammurabi, land ownership and administration had both been centralized in the temple. By Hammurabi's time, a landowning peasant class had developed. In times of disaster—flood, drought, blight or epidemic—the peasants had to borrow in order to survive. As a result, they could become the victims of crippling debts. The beginning of the reign of a new monarch might be the occasion for a general remission of debts; the reference, during Hammurabi's reign, to "the year in which he brought justice to the land" may refer to such an edict. The same reference occurs in the prologue on the stele that was quoted at the beginning of this chapter:

Then did Anu and Enlil name me,
Hammurabi, the devout, god-fearing prince,
To make justice rule in the land. . . .

That stele is the main source of what we know about Hammurabi.

When found, the stele was broken into three large blocks of diorite, a very hard and expensive stone used for royal inscriptions and important legal documents. When the blocks were put together they made a cone-shaped monument nearly eight feet high, two feet wide and measuring five feet in circumference at the head and over six feet at the base. At the head was an engraving of Shamash, sun-god and god of justice. The engraving shows Shamash seated on his throne, wearing a horned headdress and holding a scepter and ring. It appears that he is receiving homage from Hammurabi who stands before him with his right arm raised in prayer.

While this interpretation of the sculpture is generally accepted by scholars, there are others who submit varying suppositions. Some are of the opinion that Shamash is dictating the laws to the king. Others think that the king is offering the laws to the god. Still others maintain that Shamash is offering to Hammurabi the scepter and ring as the divine symbol of sovereignty which empowers him to decree laws.

Beneath and behind the god's throne begin the engraved texts of the laws in hundreds of lines arranged in columns reading from top to bottom. Parallel vertical lines and horizontal bands running round the stele, increasing in girth as they descend the column, mark off the laws so that they are well divided and do not run together. Alto-

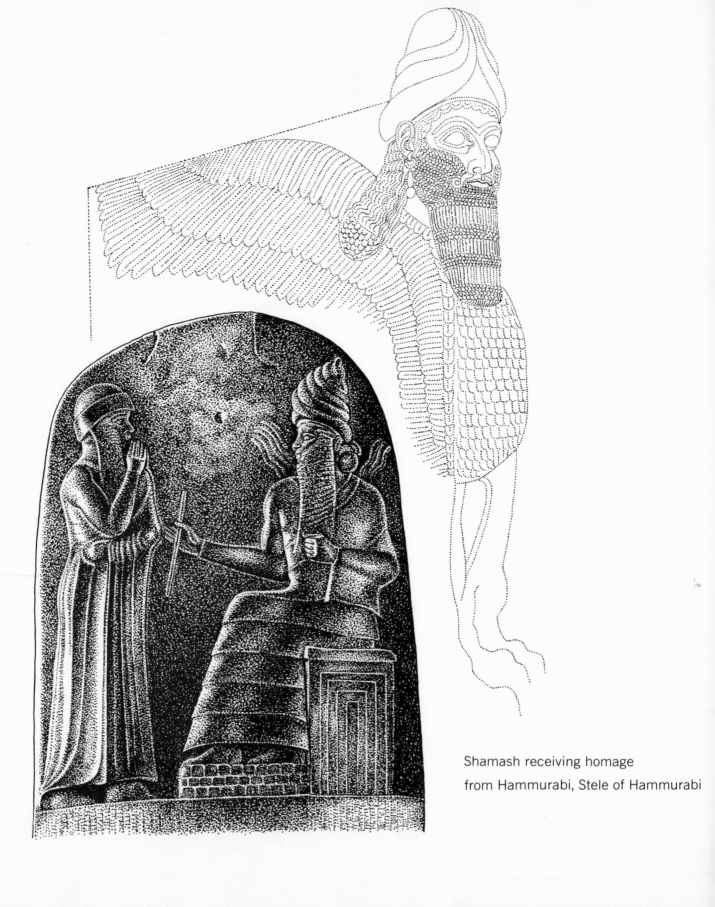

Shamash receiving homage
from Hammurabi, Stele of Hammurabi

gether the Code consists of about two hundred and twenty paragraphs covering a like number of laws. The Code is preceded by a prologue of five and a half columns, the opening lines of which are quoted at the beginning of this chapter. The prologue quoted below continues in the same exalted style:

I made an end of war
I promoted the welfare of the land.
I made the peoples rest in friendly dwellings,
I did not allow trouble-makers in their midst.
The great gods called me,
And I was the beneficent shepherd of righteous scepter,
And my benign shadow spread over my city.
I took to my bosom the peoples of Sumer and Akkad,
I have governed them in peace,
I have sheltered them with my wisdom,
That the strong might not oppress the weak,
That justice might be done to the orphan and the widow . . .
Let any oppressed man who has a cause
Come into the presence of my statue as king of justice,
Read my inscribed stele,
And give ear to my precious words;
And may my stele make clear to him his cause,
Show him his rights,
And set his mind at rest.

The inscription ends with an epilogue of five lines hurling terrible maledictions (reminiscent of those in Leviticus, chapter 26 and Deuteronomy, chapter 25) on him who pays no heed to the words engraved therein, who does not fear the gods, who abolishes the laws of the Code and substitutes others and who erases the name of Hammurabi from the stone and substitutes his own.

Fortunately, the inscription has been preserved in a singularly legible condition. Only a few lines have been erased. It appears clear that the obliteration was not the result of the hand of time but that of man. Again scholars are in debate about what happened but the more accepted theory is that a king of Elam carried off the stele in a raid on Babylon and erased a number of lines to record his own achievements. Similar erasures on two other Babylonian monuments found in Elam, which were inscribed by this king, would seem to validate this theory.

Hammurabi's greatest achievement was as an administrator and codifier of the law. Although the Code of Hammurabi was inscribed as much as a thousand years before Moses, and two thousand before the Roman Code, he was by no means the first lawgiver. It appears that many of the city-states of Mesopotamia left records of their laws, written in either Sumerian or Àkkadian. Very probably Hammurabi drew upon such documents, and the style of his own Code may even have been based upon them. Its language is Akkadian, a language related to Hebrew and Arabic, which by his time had become the priestly language of cult and ritual.

The Code of Hammurabi is also one of the most important social documents that archeology has ever uncovered. It deals with a wide range of human activities—marriage and divorce, family life, property rights, military service, commerce, agriculture, inheritance—as well as murder, assault, theft and injury.

Babylonian society consisted of three classes: the patricians, who enjoyed all the rights and privileges of free citizenship; the plebians, who were subject to certain legal restrictions (for example, on the transfer of real estate or other immovable property); and the slaves, who were regarded as the chattels of their masters and were under their protection. Property rights were highly developed and well organized; written contracts and deeds of sale were usual. Both wages and prices were fixed by royal decree, along with the rates for the hiring of boats and wagons. The rule of *noblesse oblige* was generally applied; for the upper classes, penalties for wrongdoing were harsher than for the others. And the king himself was not exempt from the provisions of the law.

Of the more than two hundred clauses in the Code of Hammurabi, twenty-seven impose the death sentence; among the crimes so punished are theft, adultery and bearing false witness where the life of the defendant is involved. The death penalty also figures in the Talmudic laws—the laws of retribution. For example, Clauses 229 and 230 of the Code of Hammurabi provide that if a house collapses because of faulty workmanship and the owner is killed, the builder shall be put to death; and if the son of the owner is killed, the penalty shall fall on a son of the builder. Similarly, in Clause 196, the Code specified that if a free man injured the eye of a patrician, his own eye should be injured; and in Clause 200, that a man who knocked out the tooth of a man of his own rank should in turn have a tooth knocked out.

It appears that retaliation was a fundamental principle of ancient law. It says in the law of Moses, as recorded in Exodus 21:23-25: ". . . the penalty shall be life for life, eye for eye, tooth for tooth, hand for hand, foot for foot, burn for burn, wound for wound, bruise for bruise."

It is interesting to compare other provisions of the Code of Hammurabi with the laws recorded in the Torah. While the Hammurabi Code takes the practice of sorcerers for granted and provides certain regulations dealing with witchcraft and sorcery, the laws of Israel unequivocally banned all practices of soothsaying, consulting ghosts and any form of magic (Deuteronomy 18:10-12).

The laws concerning false witness in the two codes are fundamentally alike. Clause 3 of the Code of Hammurabi provides that a man who has borne false witness in a capital case shall be put to death; and Deuteronomy 19:16-19 provides that "if a man appears against another to testify maliciously and gives false testimony against him . . . you shall do to him as he schemed to do to his fellow. Thus you will sweep out evil from your midst. . . ."

A degree of similarity may be found in the laws governing the punishment for theft. Clause 8 of the Code of Hammurabi provides that a man who steals an animal or a boat shall pay thirtyfold, or if he is a poor man, tenfold; and that if he has nothing to pay, he shall be put to death. According to Exodus 21:37-22:3, "When a man steals an ox or a sheep, and slaughters it or sells it, he shall pay five oxen for the ox, and four sheep for the sheep. . . . He must make restitution; if he lacks the means, he shall be sold for his theft. But if what he stole — whether ox or ass or sheep — is found alive in his possession, he shall pay double."

Slavery was recognized in both ancient Israel and Babylonia, but there are striking differences in the laws concerning slaves. Clause 15 of the Code of Hammurabi provides the death penalty for anyone who aids a slave to escape; and Clause 16 assigns the same penalty to anyone harboring an escaped slave. In ancient Israel, on the other hand, the death penalty is pronounced upon anyone guilty of kidnaping a man for the purpose of selling him as a slave (Exodus 21:16); moreover, Deuteronomy 23:16 stipulates, "You shall not turn over to his master a slave who seeks refuge with you from his master." Behind the more generous attitude of the law of Moses is the reminder, in both Exodus and Leviticus and again in the Book of Deuteronomy, "that you were slaves in the land of Egypt and the Lord your God redeemed you."

The Code of Hammurabi, in Clause 23, contains a remarkable provision for the victim of robbery: if the thief is not caught, upon declaring his loss "in the presence of a god" — that is, in a temple — the victim is to be compensated by the government of the city and territory in which the theft occurred. The law of Moses contains nothing comparable.

A number of regulations in the Code of Hammurabi are concerned with irrigation, in particular with restitution for damages caused by a man's failure to keep his section of a dike in repair, or by carelessness in leaving the sluices open. In Palestine there was no irrigation; but a comparable regulation, indicating the peculiar dangers of the region, appears in Exodus 22:5: "When a fire is started and spreads to thorns, so that stacked, standing or growing grain is consumed, he who started the fire must make restitution."

Both codes deal with the depredations of sheep on land owned by others; according to Exodus 22:4, restitution must be made "according to the top yield" from the field or vineyard in question, whereas in the Code of Hammurabi the compensation is spelled out in greater detail — so much grain for such an acreage of land.

The agricultural laws of Babylonia were frequently concerned with the relations of the landlord with his tenants, a relation that was unknown in ancient Israel, where each man worked his own land. The many provisions for the poor in the Mosaic law — for example, "When you shake the fruit from your olive trees, do not go over them again; that shall go to the stranger, the fatherless and the widow," in Deuteronomy 24:20 — have no equivalent in the Code of Hammurabi. Babylonian society seems to have been wealthier, the social structure more complex and more impersonal than that in Palestine.

Imprisonment or temporary enslavement for debt is provided for by the Code of Hammurabi, and similar regulations were in force among the Israelites. Clause 117 in the Babylonian code provides that the wife, son or daughter of a man subject to attachment for debt may be sold as slaves for a period of three years; under the law of Moses, as set down in Exodus 21 and in Deuteronomy 15:12–18, Hebrew slaves were to be released at the end of six years, with special provisions for the girl whose father has sold her as a slave:

> *She shall not be freed as male slaves are. If she proves to be displeasing to her master, who had designated her for himself, he must let her be redeemed; he shall not have the right to sell her to outsiders, since he broke faith with her. And if he designated her for his son, he shall deal with her as is the practice with free*

maidens. If he marries another, he must not withhold from this one her food, her clothing or her conjugal rights. If he fails her in these three ways, she shall be freed, without payment. (Exodus 21:7–11)

Both the Bible and the Code of Hammurabi make a distinction between willful murder and accidental homicide, and impose the death penalty for the former. Under the Babylonian code, a man guilty of accidental homicide may escape the penalty by swearing that he did not intend to kill, and by paying a fine. Exodus 21:13 and Deuteronomy 19:3–5 provide that a man who has committed accidental homicide may be given sanctuary: "You shall survey the distances, and divide into three parts the territory of the country that the Lord your God has allotted to you, so that any manslayer may have a place to flee to. . . . Now this is the case of the manslayer who may flee there and live: one who has killed another unwittingly, without having been his enemy in the past." Again, the provisions of the two codes for injuries inflicted in a fight are the same: that the one who has inflicted the injury must pay for the time lost and for the services of the physician attending the injured man.

A summing up of the comparison of the biblical laws with the Code of Hammurabi teaches us that in every age the fundamental principles of justice reflect the circumstances of the life of the times yet essentially remain the same. Although there are a number of strong similarities, there are enough differences to indicate that there was no direct borrowing. The most striking difference of all is the underlying attitude toward ultimate responsibility for justice. Whatever the relief on the stele was intended to represent—the receiving or the giving of the emblems of sovereignty by Hammurabi—there can be no doubt that unlike Moses, Hammurabi took to himself the credit for having established justice. Moses claimed no such credit; for him, God alone was the source of the Law. Moreover, whereas the Code of Hammurabi is entirely secular, the biblical code not only contains many regulations dealing with worship, but is infused with the attitude of reverence for a higher authority of which Moses himself was the living embodiment.

The epoch of Hammurabi has been described as the golden age of Babylon. Not long after his death the dynasty of Hammurabi began to decline. The region was attacked in turn by the Hittites and the Kassites, the latter possibly ancestors of the Kurds, a people found in Iraq today. Then it was the turn of the Assyrians, under Tiglath Pileser III, who in 728 B.C. had himself crowned emperor in Babylon. In the year 612 B.C., the ancient capital of Hammurabi once again became the center of a great military power, with Nebuchadnezzar as its ruler.

When the excavations of ancient Babylon were begun in 1899 by German archeologists, under the direction of Robert Koldewey, it was Nebuchadnezzar's sumptuous capital, with its palaces and hanging gardens, its great bridges, massive walls and broad avenues paved with marble, that the archeologists dug up. Of the city of Hammurabi, scarcely a trace remained except for the Code, which had been carried off by the Elamites, finally to be unearthed at Susa, two hundred miles away.

2

FROM PICTURES TO SYMBOLS, TO WEDGE SHAPES, TO WRITING:
The Triumph of the Alphabet

Writing is the counterpart of speech and has made possible the communication of the culture of mankind. It began in embryonic forms in various parts of the world and did not develop into any systematic form before the middle of the fourth millennium B.C. in Palestine or Syria. The script invented there became the basis for Greek, Latin, Slavic, and other Indo-European alphabets.

Throughout the world, the nature of the earliest known written communication was fundamentally the same, whether drawn on bark or skin, incised in clay, carved in stone or painted on the walls of a cave. And the same sort of embryonic writing still functions to this day. Traveling by car in a foreign country whose language is unknown to us, we nevertheless understand that a raised palm means *stop,* that an arrow indicates a turn in the road, that a picture of tracks means we are near a railroad crossing, and so on. These ideographs, or symbols, that denote the same meaning regardless of the language spoken, are indispensable. They represent the simplest form of written communication independent of any language.

A more advanced state, but still rudimentary, in the development of writing, appears on the ancient Egyptian obelisks (tapering four-sided shafts of stone) that may be seen in Central Park in New York City (Cleopatra's Needle), in the Place de la Concorde in Paris and at the center of Istanbul, among other places. Incised on these towering shafts are pictured objects which represent words or syllables, rather than things. Such symbolic characters (or sense signs) are called pictograms. Sense signs that stand for an action, or connote an abstract idea or quality, are called ideograms. For example, an eagle may stand for swiftness, a lion for strength and a handclasp for friendship. The development from the stage of concrete representation to abstract symbol was, of course, a process covering many centuries. It was still a far cry from a complete system.

These symbols are independent of speech. There is no connection between the symbol and the spoken name for it. It could be read in any language. A more advanced stage is the phonogram, or sound sign, a sign representing not an idea but a sound. Thus, for example, the coat of arms of the city of Oxford, England, shows an ox crossing a ford. This is a phonogram illustrating symbols representing speech connected with a specific language. The phonogram in its most advanced form is represented by the Hebrew alphabet (see page 24). The Egyptians themselves developed a rudimentary system of this sort, including some twenty-four signs that stood for separated single consonants. Thus in some Egyptian writing a hieroglyph (a pictorial character) is not necessarily a pictograph; it may also be one of these consonantal sounds or phonograms—a fact that anyone who sets out to decipher an ancient Egyptian text must always bear in mind. If the Egyptians had gone on to adopt the use of phonograms exclusively, they would have invented an alphabet of their own. But they never did, and we do not know exactly why. Indeed for many centuries in Egypt, pictograms, ideograms and phonograms existed in the same system side by side. (See page 24, #2.)

At first the Egyptians carved on stone, producing what is known as monumental writing. The advantage of this laborious, time-consuming and elegant form is its almost eternal durability; its disadvantage was in being costly and slow, so that its use was restricted to royalty and the priestly caste.

As cities grew and trade and commerce advanced, writing became more widespread. A very different material from stone was needed and soon came into general use. This was the papyrus made from a reed that grew abundantly on the banks of the Nile River. The pith from its stems, sliced and flattened into sheets, became the earliest form of paper, and gave that common writing material its name. Writing was done with a quill, or a sharpened stem from the papyrus itself, and ink was made from vegetable gum, soot and water. The materials used influenced the type of writing instrument required. The script used for writing on papyrus became very different from the carved symbols which composed the earliest picture writing. A running or cursive form developed. First was the hieratic system (from the Greek *hiereus* meaning "priest") used for religious purposes and in royal documents, and later the demotic manner (from the Greek word *demos,* meaning "people"). The demotic form was used more and more as the services of scribes were needed to check bills of lading, keep financial accounts and records, etcetera, which required speed, efficiency and convenience. Inevitably, the symbols lost their pictorial and monumental character. Writing became a popular art and a noble profession.

Fortunately for our knowledge of antiquity, the dry climate of Egypt preserved many of these papyri, which had been stored in underground tombs and temple vaults over thousands of years. The style adopted by the scribes ultimately also affected the writing carved on monuments and on such unique treasures as the Rosetta Stone,[1] the key to the decipherment of the Egyptian script.

Far to the east of the Nile, in the fertile region of Mesopotamia, another form of writing developed—one less picturesque than the Egyptian, but destined to have a far greater influence on the development of the alphabet. It was the first systematic script and represented a great leap in history similar to the discovery of the wheel and fire or the "giant leap for mankind" when Neil Armstrong made his first step on the moon. It used as a writing material neither the stone nor the papyrus of Egypt, but the clay that had been abundantly deposited by the great Tigris and Euphrates Rivers.

In the region of Sumer, near the Persian Gulf, this clay became the chief building material in the highly developed civilization that flourished between the two rivers; made into tablets, it also provided the material for concluding contracts and commercial transactions. Many scholars believe that the earliest form of business communication consisted of carved stone cylinder seals which, pressed into wet clay, left

[1] See "The Riddle of the Rosetta Stone" and "Secret Codes and Forgotten Languages," *Worlds Lost and Found,* Azriel Eisenberg and Dov Peretz Elkins (Abelard-Schuman, New York, 1964).

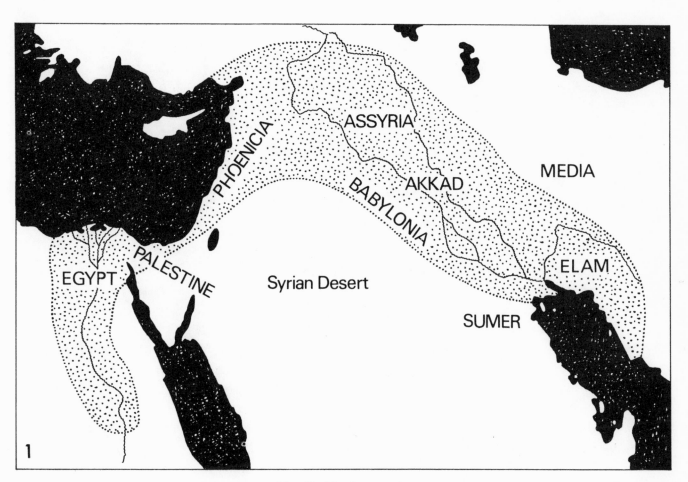

The Fertile Crescent

an impression that served as a label or signature for the merchandise that was intended for trade and export. Eventually, entire documents were incised on wet clay.

Originally, the Sumerians used a form of picture writing, using a pointed stylus, made from a reed, as a tool; then, to facilitate the work of the scribe, a stylus was designed with a triangular tip that left a wedge-shaped mark. It is from the Latin word *cuneus* meaning "wedge" that the writing of ancient Mesopotamia got its name—cuneiform. Instead of the connected strokes of ordinary cursive writing, cuneiform characters were made up entirely of these wedge-shaped marks combined in various ways. Although this sounds to us like an extremely awkward way of writing, the Sumerian and later the Babylonian scribe worked with remarkable speed and deftness, holding the soft clay tablet in his left palm while he pressed down the stylus with his right, turning the wedge to point up, down or sideways as he formed the letter. As in Hebrew, the line read from right to left, and in the marks placed crosswise, the thick end of the wedge was almost always to the left. (See page 24, #4.)

During the Assyrian empire, cuneiform writing became increasingly refined, so that each stroke denoted a single syllable. Like Latin during the Middle Ages, and French or English in more recent times, it became the *lingua franca* or international medium of communication, and was used even in Egypt. But the alphabet as we know it was still in the future.

According to Dr. David Diringer in his authoritative book, *The Story of the Aleph Bet,* "We may date the origin of the alphabet about 1800–1700 B.C. . . . The political situation of the Old World at that period favored the creation of a 'revolutionary,' 'democratic' writing in contradistinction to the 'conservative,' 'theocratic' scripts of the old states of Mesopotamia and Egypt." [2]

What appears to be the earliest forerunner of the alphabet was discovered in 1905 at Serabit, in the Sinai Peninsula, not far from Mount Sinai, where mining was carried on by Semitic slaves under Egyptian overseers. Archeologists and scholars are of the opinion that the system of writing used there developed out of the need for a kind of shorthand for recording the output of the mines, and that it was the result of a kind of cross-fertilization of Egyptian hieroglyphs with the North-Semitic cuneiform. It consisted of thirty-two or thirty-four signs; some scholars have reduced it to twenty-four by eliminating the variants. This low number of signs has led to the theory that it must be an alphabet. Estimates of the date of this earliest alphabetic writing vary from 1850–1500 B.C.

Another inscription in alphabetic characters, dating to 1300 B.C., was discovered in 1922 at the site of Byblos, north of Beirut in what is now Lebanon. Byblos played an important role in the history of writing since it was an export center for papyrus. The Greeks who imported this material called it *byblos* from which came the word bible or book. There have been other such discoveries since 1922 and in all of them, the writing is made up of between twenty and thirty symbols, each representing a sound uttered by the human voice. Most scholars now believe that writing of this sort was already being used in Canaan at the time of Abraham. It is also agreed that this system was the forerunner not only of the Semitic Hebrew alphabet, but also of the Greek alphabet, and thus of the Latin and Cyrillic (Russian and Slavic) alphabets used in

[2] This and the quotations that follow are from David Diringer's *The Story of the Aleph Bet,* Thomas Yoseloff, 1960.

Europe and throughout the Western world today.[3]

Dr. Diringer writes that the territory in which the original development of writing took place was a melting pot in which were mingled "the influences from the northeast (Mesopotamia) and the southwest (Egypt), from the north (the Hittites) and the west (the Minoan civilization).[4] Having received various elements of culture from the surrounding countries, the northwest Semites handed them on, somewhat elaborated and transformed, to other contiguous regions. . . . Moreover, the language spoken in this region was particularly favorable to the creation of a consonantal alphabet." Each of the twenty-two symbols in the North-Semitic alphabet represents a consonant; there are no vowels. What made the new system unique was that for the first time each sound was represented by a particular sign. "For this achievement, simple as it is," says Dr. Diringer, "the inventor is to be ranked among the greatest benefactors of mankind."

The way in which the development of systematic writing took place is made clearer by an examination of the Hebrew alphabet. One widely held theory is the so-called acrophonic (from the Greek word *akron,* meaning "highest" or "outermost") account of its origin. According to this theory, the sound represented by each character corresponds to the beginning sound in a word which that character depicts. For example, gimel, the third letter in the Hebrew alphabet, stands for camel (gamal in Hebrew). From the accompanying illustration, it may be seen that with a little imagination the strokes composing the letter can call up the mental image of the reclining body of a camel. (See page 24.)

[3] In each of these alphabets, the order is comparable to that of the tablets in Ugaritic cuneiform (a North Canaanite dialect akin to the Hebrew of the pre-Mosaic era), that have been discovered on the north Syrian coast, and that have been dated to the second millennium B.C. The order of the Hebrew alphabet written from right to left is listed acrostically in

Similarly, the letter beth is derived from bayith, meaning "house"; and its rectangular outlines do suggest the shape of a house. The letter daleth comes from deleth, the word for "door"; and the shape suggests an entrance way.

It will be noted that all the objects thus represented come from everyday life. Each sound is represented by one sign, and a combination of signs makes up a syllable and/or word. Consisting of twenty-two letters expressing consonants, the Hebrew alphabet has been read and written from right to left from ancient times until this day. There are no capital and small letters (majuscule and miniscule). We are not certain whether the letters were originally pictographic, giving the name of the object to the aleph-bet, or the names were applied to the letters later, unrelated to what they represented.

For those who hold the latter theory, Dr. Diringer raises a startling and intriguing question: Did the Second Commandment, prohibiting the making of images or a likeness of anything, play a role in the invention of the alphabet as a non-representational system in contrast to the original non-alphabetic writing which was representational? The Ten Commandments were promulgated about the fourteenth century B.C. and the alphabet invented about three hundred years earlier. Nevertheless the ideas of the faith of Israel were much older than their consummation in the Ten Commandments. It is possible that along with the great revolutionary ideas of monotheism and the Bible, the Hebrews (and their North-Semitic neighbors) also contributed the extraordinary invention of a non-representational alphabet which laid the bases of Western civilization and culture.

The derivation of the Greek alphabet, "the earliest fully developed alphabetic sys-

Lamentations 1–4, Proverbs 31:10–131, Psalms 25, 34, 91, 92, and elsewhere in the Hebrew Bible.
    [4] Greek culture of the Bronze Age in Crete, 3000–1100 B.C.

2

3

Egyptian hieroglyph

Gimel-camel, the third letter of the Hebrew alphabet

4

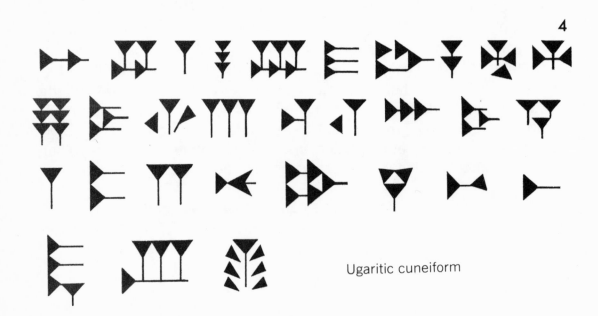

Ugaritic cuneiform

tem of writing containing both consonants and vowels," is clear and accepted by scholars. The shape of the letters is derived from the Hebrew and North-Semitic characters. The phonetic value of most of the characters is the same. So is the order (aleph, bet, gimel, daleth, etc.—alpha, beta, gamma, delta, etc.). The names are derived from the Semitic value as indicated above. Since they have meaning in Semitic and no meaning in Greek, it seems clear that they are borrowed. Early Greek was also written from right to left and changed centuries later. The alphabet came to them through the great sea traders of the time, the Phoenicians.

The Latin script like the Latin language swept over all the countries of the Roman empire, and out of it grew the modern romance languages: Italian, French, Spanish, Portuguese and Roumanian.

3

THE FAT OLD KING WHO CONQUERED ISRAEL:
The Story of the Merneptah Stele

In December 1895, Sir Flinders Petrie, a distinguished British archeologist, arrived in Egypt. He had conducted digs there for many years. This time he turned his attention to Thebes, a glorious ancient city, once the residence of royalty, and the seat of worship of the god Amon.

Many parts of Thebes, particularly the cemeteries, had already been ransacked by treasure hunters. But there was a complex of temples of the Pharaohs, along the desert edge of the western shore of the city, which lay undisturbed. In this district, a half-mile long, were six temples of ancient Egyptian kings.

On December 16, 1895, digging began. Petrie had hired local farmers to do the actual labor. Living close by, they would have only a short walk to work and could return home for meals and lodging, which simplified Petrie's organizational problems.

A few mornings after work began, Petrie noticed a stranger walking among the ruins.

The newcomer began to whisper something to the government official who had been assigned to the dig to make sure that all finds were divided fairly between Petrie and the Egyptian government. Watching this, Petrie's curiosity became aroused and he made some inquiries. Finding that the stranger was a dealer of antiquities from Cairo, he became suspicious.

"What do you have in your briefcase?" asked the archeologist.

"Nothing," said the man, who quickly turned to leave. As he began to hurry away, his suitcase dropped and fell open. There on the ground lay the evidence. He had purchased some of the small finds from the government official. Instead of guarding the finds for the Department of Antiquities, the official was selling some of them and keeping the profits for himself. Without hesitation, Petrie ordered the official off the dig. From then on, the archeological team worked without government "supervision."

A few weeks later a second problem came to light. This time the workers themselves were at fault. Petrie's assistants, Jeffe Haworth and Martyn Kennard, noticed some minor finds, such as pottery, had disappeared. After an investigation of the neighboring settlement, they discovered that the workers had been smuggling small finds from the excavation site, to give to their relatives and friends as presents.

On January 13, 1896, Petrie called all the workers together and fired them. He made a point of his anger, so the word would spread among the local population that he would not tolerate theft. Then he hired an entirely new crew from a village three miles away, too far to cart things to their families.

As a further step to prevent stealing, Petrie decided to sleep in the ancient temple of Thebes with his assistants.

One afternoon during the hours when the sun was hottest, Petrie and his co-workers decided to take a short nap in their quarters inside the temple. While they were sleeping some American tourists strolled by, looking among the ruins.

"Look here," called one of them. "People are still inhabiting these old temples. They are probably related to the original Pharaohs."

Petrie lifted his head from the pillow for a moment to hear the talk, laughed to himself and went back to sleep. Even during his rest hour, however, he tried to keep a watchful eye on the remains. While the dig was still in process everything lay exposed, an easy prey to souvenir hunters.

After several weeks of digging and clearing away the vast accumulation of debris that centuries had deposited within the temples, the team approached the ancient funeral temple of King Merneptah, who ruled from 1224 to 1216 B.C. It seemed the least interesting of the temples, with piles of soft sandstone cluttering its entrances and broken sphinxes, crumbling to small pieces, strewn all over the inside and outside.

"I think we'll skip this temple," said Petrie. "Its condition is too poor. Even if there is something inside, it will be too hard to get to. And more than likely everything is crushed and crumbling."

One of Petrie's associates, Dr. Wilhelm Spiegelberg of the University of Strasbourg, was of a different opinion. "It would be foolish to overlook it," said the scholar. "Let's spend a few days and if we cannot get through, we'll leave it."

Petrie consented, provided only a few days would be spent.

Three days later, in one of the entrance courts to the temple, workers uncovered pieces of a colossal seated statue of Merneptah, made of black granite. Petrie's optimism began to return. Shortly after that, another enormous statue of Merneptah appeared, quite intact. Petrie gave orders to continue work on the temple. It was obviously a better source of finds than he had expected. But he had not yet realized how important the temple really was.

Not too much later, a worker clearing the temple's first court in the southwest corner discovered a huge piece of black granite lying on the ground, and immediately summoned Dr. Petrie. Under the supervision of the chief archeologist the rest of the granite piece was uncovered. It turned out to be a stele ten feet long and five feet wide. On its surface was an inscription which Dr. Petrie asked his associate, Dr. Spiegelberg, an expert in hieroglyphics, to read.

"This is from the reign of Amenhotep III," said Spiegelberg, "who was Pharaoh during the fourteenth century B.C."

"What is it doing here?" asked Petrie, perplexed. "This is the temple of Merneptah, whose rule was in the late thirteenth century B.C."

Musing over the problem, Petrie gave orders to have the stele picked up and placed in its original upright position. The men tried to move it, but it was too heavy. They lifted it a few inches, but could not get it all the way up. Petrie bent down on his knees and glanced at the rough side of the stele. To his amazement he saw that this side also had writing on it.

"Spiegelberg, come quickly. I have the answer! This is the reason why the stele is in the temple of Merneptah. Many decades after Amenhotep III, it was reused on the reverse side. A second inscription was cut by Merneptah, and it was turned around with the original front side to the wall."

The men cut the ground away under the stele and propped it up with some stones. It was just a few inches from the ground, but Spiegelberg crawled under it and, lying on his back, began to try to read its ancient hieroglyphics.

They were extremely hard to read because the back surface of the stele was rough, not like the original front side. The Professor could make out a carved picture at the top that had retained its original colors: yellow, red and blue. The Egyptian god Amon was shown presenting a sword to Pharaoh Merneptah. With him were other Egyptian gods.

Dr. Spiegelberg lay there on his back in the dim light of the temple for hours, trying to make out the poorly carved words of the stele. That evening at the dinner table, he discussed his finds with Petrie.

"I found on the stele the names of several Syrian towns, all but one of which I was familiar with."

"Which was that?" asked Sir Flinders.

"It was something like Isirar, but I can't be certain."

"Isirar, Isirar, let's see," thought Petrie aloud, "what could it be?" Finally he ventured a suggestion. "Maybe it is Israel. I know it's a long shot, but it's close enough. Could that have been the other people mentioned on the stele?"

"Yes, that's what it must be—Israel!" Spiegelberg agreed.

"This is a tremendous find," said Petrie. "It is the first Egyptian inscription that mentions the Israelites!"

Israel

Sir Flinders Petrie and
the Merneptah Stele

Egyptian God Amon presenting a sword to Pharaoh Merneptah

That evening, Petrie confided to his friends that of all his finds, none would be better known in the world than this one, the stele of Merneptah containing the name of Israel. Even though the contents were undeciphered, Petrie sensed their importance.

After careful study Dr. Spiegelberg was able to read and translate the entire stele. It dated from the fifth year of the reign of Pharaoh Merneptah, the year 1219 B.C. The stele contained a victory song of the Pharaoh for having beaten off an attack by the Libyans and other "Sea Peoples."

Apparently one of the peoples the Pharaoh fought were the Israelites. After mentioning all the other lands Merneptah conquered in battle, the inscription states:

> *The people of Israel is laid waste,*
> *Her seed is no more.*
> *Palestine has become a widow for Egypt.*

This stele is extremely important for several reasons. First of all, it is the only known mention of the biblical Israelites in an Egyptian inscription. Second, it is the earliest mention of the Israelites in the writings of any nation. Third, it helps us pinpoint the date of the Exodus from Egypt under Moses.

The other conquered nations mentioned by Merneptah on his celebrated stele are designated as "nations" or "countries," meaning that they are settled peoples. Israel, on the other hand, is designated only as a people. This means, according to most scholars, that the Israelites in Palestine had not been there long enough to settle down.

We also know that the Israelites were in Egypt in the year 1290 B.C., when they built store cities for Pharaoh Ramses II (Exodus 1:11). Thus, it must be between 1290 and 1220 B.C., the year of the stele, that they left Egypt. Since it took them forty years to reach the Promised Land, they could not have left before 1260 B.C. The Exodus from Egypt must therefore be dated somewhere between 1290 and 1260 B.C. It is remarkable to be able to pinpoint so specifically the date of such an ancient event.

Several excavated cities in Palestine, such as Hazor and probably Lachish, were destroyed around the year 1220 B.C. This dates Joshua's conquest of the land at the same time as the Merneptah stele, giving further confirmation for the date of the Exodus and the conquest.

Merneptah's reign lasted only eight years (1224–1216 B.C.). The long and glorious reign of his father Ramses II had lasted through most of the thirteenth century (1290–1224 B.C.). When Ramses II died, his son Merneptah was almost sixty years old. From the study of his embalmed body, found in the Valley of the Kings at Thebes, medical scientists have concluded that he was a fat, bald-headed man. His death, they surmise, was caused by hardening of the arteries.

Since his reign was so short, this victory in his fifth year as king turned out to be the most important event of that reign. He exaggerated his victory somewhat, declaring that Israel had been utterly destroyed. As it turned out, Israel survived that battle and many more after.

In modern times this stele also had its part to play in history. It now stands in the Cairo Museum, Piece Number 34025. When Egypt attacked Israel in 1948, the Egyptian government issued a postage stamp with the Merneptah Stele quoted on it: "Israel is laid waste, her seed is no more. Palestine has become a widow for Egypt."

In the tradition of their ancient ancestors, the modern Egyptians were a bit too boastful. They lost the war.

4

HAZOR, THE HEAD OF ALL THOSE KINGDOMS:
A Dig That Will Take Eight Hundred Years

August 1, 1955. Archeologist Yigael Yadin stood atop the ancient mound of Hazor, nine miles north of the Sea of Galilee, and directed the excavators to clear an area where he thought a gate lay buried. As the workmen proceeded, Yadin glanced at a piece of paper and indicated to the men exactly where to dig. He told them to unearth the sides of the entrance way. "There will be three chambers on each side," he said, and proceeded to give them the dimensions. As the men continued to dig, they saw that his figures were correct.

Finally, when the entire gate complex was uncovered, they had exposed chambers, towers, an entrance passage and stone walls, all with the dimensions predicted by Yadin.

The secret lay in the pages of the Bible, as do many other archeological clues to the past. Professor Yadin, of the Hebrew University in Jerusalem, was following the verse in I Kings 9:15: "And this is the reason for the taxes which King Solomon levied, to build the house of the Lord and to build . . . Hazor, Megiddo, and Gezer." After the destruction of Hazor in Joshua's time, King Solomon rebuilt it as one of his royal cities, using it as a store city for his army and chariots.

Excavations at Megiddo, after World War I, had revealed a large gate consisting of six chambers, three on either side, with square towers for guards to watch those who wished to enter the walled city. Knowing of the Megiddo gate, Yadin reasoned that if King Solomon built both cities, Hazor probably had the same type of gate, one large enough for a chariot to enter. After Yadin's predictions proved accurate, he concluded that not only had both gates been built at the direction of King Solomon, but that both Hazor and Megiddo had been built by the same royal architect. The Bible's historical memory was amazingly correct.

The excavation at Hazor, from 1955–1959, was one of the largest and best organized digs of modern times. This dig was known as the "James A. de Rothschild Expedition at Hazor," in honor of the wealthy Englishman who financed it in behalf of the Hebrew University. It was headed by Yigael Yadin in his capacity as a member of the University Faculty of Archeology.

Professor Yadin, formerly known as General Yadin, had been Chief of Operations during Israel's War of Independence in 1948 and later Chief of Staff of the Israeli Defense Forces. The excavations he directed at Hazor have been hailed all over the world as some of the most significant of modern times, and as a model of what such undertakings should be.

In addition to expert archeologists, the excavation staff included two hundred laborers, many architects, photographers, draftsmen and archeological students. The Israeli Army also helped. Jeeps and other military vehicles were used around the mound and walkie-talkies provided instant communication with all staff members when an important find was made. Israeli Air Force crews photographed the mound from the air, providing good overall pictures of the dig as it progressed.

The tell (an Arabic word meaning artificial mound or hill) of Hazor is in the shape of a large bottle consisting of forty-five acres. Compared to Megiddo's fifteen acres, it is a large tell created by successive layers of habitations one upon the other. Over to the north, below the tell, lies a large rectangular plain of about one hundred fifty acres. This vast area makes Hazor the largest city of ancient Palestine. The upper part, or the mound, is called the Acropolis. It was occupied for more than 2500 years — from 2700 to 150 B.C. In other words, from Canaanite times, the period of the Bible, through to postbiblical Maccabean days.

The lower city, on the plain below and to the north of the hill, was used for a shorter period, during the Canaanite era, from about 1700 to 1200 B.C. It must have housed the overflow population.

Professor Yadin found as many as twenty-one different cities piled one above the other. This is the way ancient people built their cities: when one was destroyed or abandoned, another was built directly on top of it.

General Yadin was not the first to dig at Hazor. There had been a small investigation in 1928 executed by John Garstang, the English archeologist. But this was a minor dig, called soundings (trial excavations), and Garstang's notes were lost when his Manches-

Yigael Yadin with his finds at Hazor

ter home in England was bombed during World War II. Thus he was never able to publish any reports which could have helped later scholars.

Garstang's main objective in 1928 was to find out the date of Joshua's conquest of the Holy Land. He thought, incorrectly, that it took place about 1400 B.C. Hazor was certainly the place to investigate this date, for the Bible states that Joshua destroyed Hazor, a Canaanite capital, and if the date of its destruction could be fixed, then the date of Joshua's battle could be determined.

The story is told in Joshua, chapter 11. Jabin, king of Hazor, invited a group of Canaanite kings in the north to fight against the Israelites. The Canaanites comprised some eleven peoples whose territory extended from the Nile to the Euphrates (Gen. 10:15–19). Joshua killed all of them at a place known as the waters of Merom: "And Joshua turned back at that time, and took Hazor, and smote the king thereof with the sword; for Hazor was formerly the head of all those kingdoms . . . and Joshua burnt Hazor with fire." (Joshua 11:10–11)

This was a major battle in the conquest of the Holy Land. As the Bible says, "Hazor was formerly the head (capital) of all those kingdoms." That is, all the Canaanite kingdoms of northern Palestine were under her jurisdiction. After the capture, Hazor became part of the Israelite territories. It was given to the tribe of Naphtali for an inheritance.

The controversy about the date of the Exodus from Egypt and of Joshua's conquest had been raging for centuries. Dates had been suggested ranging anywhere from the fifteenth to the twelfth century B.C. Yadin's findings proved that Hazor was destroyed in the second half of the thirteenth century B.C. In addition, many other cities excavated in Palestine, and mentioned in the Bible as having been destroyed by Joshua and the twelve tribes of Israel, also show indications of destruction around this date: these include Jericho, Lachish, Bethel and Debir. When a final exact date for the Exodus is accepted, the finds at Hazor will have played an important role in its determination.

The finds during the four seasons of digging were certainly rewarding and exciting. The Rothschild Expedition staff exhumed a Canaanite temple from the fourteenth century B.C., which shed a new light on Solomon's architects. One of the pre-Israelite temples they found resembled very closely the architecture of King Solomon's famous temple in Jerusalem. The three-room plan was the prototype for the temple built some centuries later. In addition, this Canaanite temple had two pillars in the front room, resembling those described in the Bible and called Jachin and Boaz. This was the only temple found that was built before Solomon's day. Also dug up were temples to the sun-god and the moon-god. It appears that there may have been as many as 40,000 people in this Canaanite city.

It is hoped that digging will one day resume at Hazor. At the time of the first dig, Yigael Yadin was hoping to find the royal archives of the kings of Canaan. Since Hazor was "the head of all those kingdoms," it would be the natural place to keep the royal cuneiform documents, written in Sumerian and Akkadian, the *lingua franca* prior to the Israelite conquest of Canaan.

It will probably never be possible to finish excavating the entire mound at Hazor. Archeology today is a very exact, painstaking and expensive science. In its early days, explorers and treasure seekers were eager to lay their hands on valuable and spectacular objects. They destroyed the sites they had dug up, leaving no traces of the life style of the ancient civilizations uncovered.

Today a dig is planned to the last detail. Once permissions are obtained from the owners of the site and the government, a very elaborate organization is set up. Financing is very costly. The dig may be supported by private funds, the government, a university or a combination of these, as has been the case of Hazor. The staff consists of many specialists and technicians and requires vast equipment. Some of the experts needed are: an engineer, an architect, a photographer, a draftsman, scholars of ancient languages, an expert recorder, and special personnel as the expedition may dictate. The diggers are organized almost like a small army, each responsible for specific work in designated areas. In addition, there is, of course, a full commissary, an office force, and accommodations and facilities.

After a contour map is made of the surroundings, the site is marked off like a checkerboard and recorded on a map. The findings in each sector are photographed, illustrated, measured carefully and described. The goal is that after an area is dug up (and hence destroyed), it can be reconstructed from the written record of the dig, the photographs, diagrams, illustrations and so on. It is the record of past civilizations and cultures that the archeologists are after. The objects, valuable though they may be, are secondary insofar as they help illustrate the life and times of the place studied. If we take the sum of the area of excavations during the four seasons of 1955–1959, and compare it to the total area of ancient Hazor, and then calculate on that basis, it should take about eight hundred years to finish the job completely.

5

AN ARCHEOLOGIST GOES TO COURT:
Excavations of King Saul's Palace at Gibeah

In 1922, when William Foxwell Albright, Director of the American School of Oriental Research in Jerusalem, decided to dig at a mound three miles north of Jerusalem, the British government's Department of Antiquities gave him permission without any delay. His difficulties arose when he began to negotiate the other formality — leasing of the property on which the tell was located.

This was an experience which Albright would never forget. He later confessed that he had spent more time negotiating with the owners than he did in the whole excavation itself.

Why so much difficulty? It seems that this mound was not owned by a single individual but by sixty-six different shareholders in the neighborhood. This shareholding plan was common in Palestine at that time. To further complicate matters, some of the sixty-six shares were owned by one or more families.

Where to begin? Albright was determined to get the lease signed, because he wanted to end a long controversy concerning this mound which the Arabs called Tell el-Ful (Mound of Horsebeans). He wanted to prove that this was the site of the biblical city of Gibeah (the hill), where King Saul reigned as the first king of Israel. To Albright the location seemed right, and the size appropriate. All the evidence he had amassed indicated that this tell was the ancient city of King Saul. But, as in other cases, scholars disagreed. Part of the problem consisted of the fact that two biblical towns, Gibeah and Geba, lay only a few miles apart. What is more, the Bible mentions three places named Gibeah: Gibeah of Benjamin, Gibeah of Saul and Gibeah of God.

But years of living in Palestine and studying the Bible and archeology convinced Albright that Tell el-Ful was Gibeah of Saul, and that the same place was called Gibeah of Benjamin on other occasions. Eager to prove his theory correct, Albright would not let any legal technicality prevent him from excavating. He thought of a plan whereby he would persuade the owners to cooperate with him and sign a lease. He had to hire about forty laborers to assist with the digging, so he engaged some of the people who owned the land. This, he reasoned, would quiet their objections. In addition, he put the owners' representative, Mohammed 'Abd el-Haqq, in the position of foreman. This worked for a while, but not for long. The shareholders, mostly illiterate peasants, had heard tales about archeologists over the course of the past fifty years in their native Palestine. They thought the goal of archeology was to find expensive treasures buried under the soil, and they wanted a "cut of the riches." When it came time to make final negotiations, they demanded one thousand dollars for renting the property.

This was an exorbitant sum, since the American School of Oriental Research had appropriated only one thousand dollars for the entire excavation.

Professor Albright had a greal deal of patience in dealing with the native peasants. He decided to speak to each one of the shareholders individually in the presence of the district officer, Ruhi Bey. Finally they came to terms and the work resumed.

But this time another snag appeared. So determined were these shrewd farmers to grab a fat slice of the archeological pie, that they hired a dishonest lawyer from the city to come and speak for them. The episode that followed the arrival of this attorney marks an interesting but frustrating chapter in the history of archeology.

Dr. Albright opened his mail one morning to find a letter from the district court of Jerusalem:

> *Dear Sir:*
> *You are to report to the district court on Monday next to answer to the charges made against you by the owners of Tell el-Ful. Please appear with counsel representing you.*
>
> *Percy J. Granville, Judge*

This was the last straw. He almost decided to give up. No tell, he thought, was worth going to court for, even if it contained King Saul's palace itself!

At court the greedy owners made the worst sorts of charges. But the Jerusalem judge, accustomed to such money seeking, saw fit not only to exonerate the archeologist, but to admonish the owners as well. They returned to their homes to think up new schemes.

Work continued off and on during that year and the next, and by August 1923, when the first phase of the dig was completed, about forty days altogether had been spent in excavations. It was not until 1933, ten years later, that Albright found an opportunity to return to Tell el-Ful and put in another month of digging. All told, the total amount of work time came to about three months, and only two thousand dollars were spent. Compared with other digs, on which ten or twenty years were spent, and hundreds of thousands of dollars invested, the results of this excavation were sensational.

Albright determined in his short but carefully executed expedition that Tell el-Ful was occupied during the same period of time as the biblical city of Gibeah, as recorded in the Bible. In other words, it was almost certain that this tell was indeed the site of Gibeah of Saul.

The city was occupied by the early Israelites just after the conquest of the Holy Land under Joshua in the last quarter of the thirteenth century B.C. The investigation showed that the site was destroyed in the twelfth century, during the period of the Judges. It was in this very period, during an intertribal war among the Israelites, that "the whole city went up in smoke to heaven," according to the Bible (Judges 20:40). This was no doubt the event that caused the layer of ashes found by Albright on the twelfth century B.C. occupation level at Gibeah—a striking confirmation of biblical history.

However important this was, the next discovery made by the expedition was one that has been called even more remarkable and romantic.

When the workers reached the level containing the remains of the late eleventh century, the walls of a fortress began to appear. It was a small building, larger than the ordinary house of its day, but certainly not as big as a palace or royal residence. No king of Egypt or Assyria would be content to live in a building of those modest proportions. The biggest room, for example, was no larger than the average living room of a modern home. True, the pottery was a bit more luxurious than that of the average Israelite abode in the eleventh century, and the thirty cooking pots found in the kitchen indicated that some kind of important official had occupied the fortress. But it still did not seem to be the sought after palace of King Saul.

Was Albright mistaken? Was Saul's royal residence not to be found on Tell el-Ful? The diggers seemed to think the archeologist was in error, and they expressed their disappointment to him.

Further digging revealed basement storerooms which held wine, oil and grain. Then a collapsed stairway in the ruins was uncovered, indicating the existence of a second floor. Still, this was not enough to prove that a member of the royalty had occupied this building.

All during these findings Albright did not lose confidence; it was just what he expected. The fact that the site was occupied during the periods when, according to the Bible, Gibeah was the scene of activity, proved that this was Gibeah of Saul. In archeology, one is successful when the finds meet expectations, even if they are not materially spectacular.

Albright explained this to his assistants. "All this simplicity makes the discovery even more dramatic," he said to them. "What we have unearthed here at Tell el-Ful fits exactly the picture of King Saul which we have from the Bible."

King Saul was a tall, handsome and stately man. But he was essentially a warrior, a tribal hero, who was elevated to the new post of king when the Philistine threat required united action on the part of all of the twelve tribes of Israel.

Saul was a king equal to the situation. What the tribes needed was a physically impressive individual who could lead them in battle against the enemy. They did not need, nor could they afford, a complicated bureaucracy of government, nor a lavishly built royal palace. The mark of Saul was basically a "rustic simplicity." He was—and remained—a comfortable landowner. When he became king there was no change in administration of the tribes. His only officer was his cousin Abner. Neither did he maintain a kingly court. His army was only a modest one. What he did was to maintain his own home town as the new capital of organized Israel. He built there what can better be described as a fortress than a palace.

It was a very inspiring thing for Albright's archeological team to stand on the ruins of this ancient building. They were filled with pride when they knew that they had unearthed the birthplace of the kingdom of Israel.

"Gibeah was located at a strategic place," Albright told the laborers one night after the "palace" had been uncovered. "Being close to many important biblical sites, Saul was able to stand in its high watchtowers and observe the many battles which took place during his reign." As the archeologist spoke, he pointed to the palace which everyone could see reconstructed in his mind's eye.

"It was to this 'palace,'" he continued, "that young David came to sing sweet songs and soothe his troubled king with the melodious sounds of his harp."

Albright continued in a dramatic voice, "And it was from here that the tragic king marched towards Mount Gilboa, where, trying to defend his kingdom from the Philistines, he saw his last battle."

David playing the harp for King Saul

The excavations showed that the building was not destroyed after Saul's death. Perhaps some loyal member of the former king's family saw to it that the fortress was not completely demolished. But it is likely that the Philistines left the place in an unusable condition, for it was not inhabited again for two hundred years. Under David's strong hand the Philistine menace was ended, and the capital moved to larger head-quarters at Jerusalem. The fortress of Gibeah had outlived its usefulness. Gibeah was occupied again in the eighth century B.C., but the Judean fortress at that time was even smaller than King Saul's.

Much can be deduced about life during the eighth century in this small village from its pottery. There was little variety (Albright called it monotonously uniform) and it consisted mainly of bowls. No cooking pots were found, and Albright concluded from this that a military garrison was probably stationed there at the time, and that the fortress was only important for its watchtower. There was no luxury, merely the plain-ness of regimented military life. Everyone had the same type bowl and ate the same plain food.

Any find that comes after discovering the palace of the first king of Israel must seem insignificant. And so we shall close this story by saying that the village of Gibeah, once occupied by a king and warrior, was destroyed in A.D. 70 by the Roman Commander Titus on his way to capture Jerusalem. There he destroyed the Temple and burned the holy city to the ground.

The money spent on the Gibeah excavation was negligible, the time short, the effort and political entanglement great, but the finds were amazing. Even worth going to court for.

6

THE ANCIENT WEIGHT THAT SOLVED A PUZZLE:
The Story of How a Biblical Verse Came to Life

Under the blazing Jerusalem sun, a young schoolboy, Shahib, was walking along slowly with his friends. The year was 1902, the time early summer. School had just let out until fall, and Shahib and his friends decided to go on a picnic. They were carefully clothed in head-coverings and white shirts and slacks so they would not become overexposed to the sun.

Suddenly Shahib heard a ringing noise as his foot kicked a metal object. He bent over to look at it, with his back to the glaring sun. His friends crouched around him, craning their necks to see what he had found.

The object, whatever it was, was made of a brassy bronze. Shahib reached into his pocket, took out a handkerchief, and rubbed the dirt from its surface. As he did so, he thought of Aladdin and the magic lamp. He almost expected a genie to appear as he brushed and buffed it. He was only partially disappointed. There was no genie, but the

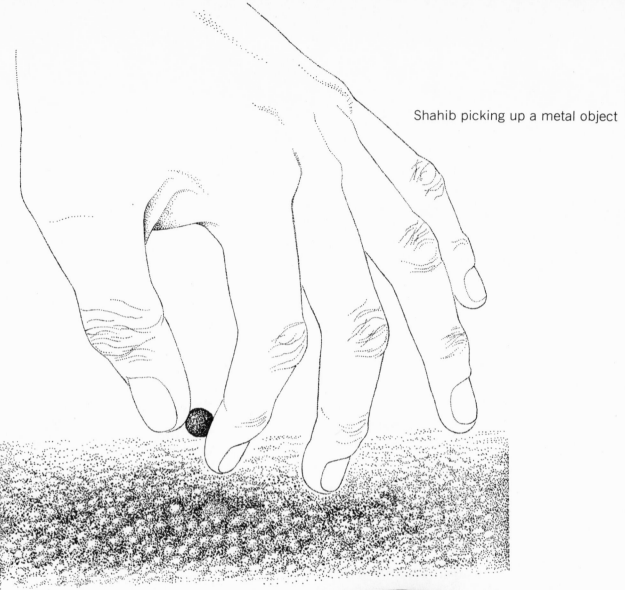

Shahib picking up a metal object

The word "Pim" and a "Pim" weight

discovery proved to be of great interest. Scratched on the surface of the bronze object were some strangely shaped characters.

"This must be . . ." he started to exclaim excitedly.

He immediately stopped himself. What if this is valuable? he thought. I had better be careful not to seem too excited. If I keep the secret to myself, I'll be able to get the entire reward.

"Ah, it's nothing," he said to his friends to distract their interest. "Just a piece of a baby's game, or something like that." Then, with a shrewd maneuver of his hands, he picked up a stone while no one saw him and threw it away, pretending it was the piece of metal he had just discovered.

"Come on, we'll be late for the picnic." And the group went on.

All that day, Shahib concealed his excitement, and his hope that he had found some significant object worth lots of money. "No one must know until I have sold it," he whispered to himself.

The next day, when his friends called on him to go outside to play ball, Shahib told them he wasn't feeling well. His friends went to play without him. When Shahib thought they had walked a considerable distance, he peered out of the window, trying not to let himself be seen. He waited a few more minutes, and then went upstairs to his bedroom. There he reached into a drawer and pulled out a pair of green socks and slowly rolled out the piece of metal he had hidden there the day before.

He sighed with relief. It's still here. I must now bring it over to my father's friend, Mr. Dushoff, the antiquities dealer.

As he left through the back door, Shahib was very careful not to be seen by anyone who knew him. He did not want to have to stop on the way and get involved in a conversation about the purpose of his mission.

Finally he arrived at Mr. Dushoff's store. Slowly and carefully he took out the piece of bronze with the writing on it.

"Yes, Shahib, this certainly is an ancient piece of metal, and although I can't read it, I recognize this as ancient Hebrew writing. I'll be glad to purchase it from you." Shahib's face gleamed with joy. He would now be able to buy himself the set of building tools he had always wanted.

A few days later in that same summer of 1902, an American Bible scholar, Professor George A. Barton from Bryn Mawr College, Pennsylvania, came into Mr. Dushoff's antiquities store to browse around. Mr. Dushoff showed him the metal object, along with some other objects—some round, some rectangular, some stone, some metal. Professor Barton decided to take them all.

The stage was now set for the great discovery to be made. A tiny object which may just as easily have been kicked into a pile of rubbish and never recovered had landed in the study of an expert who had come from a country thousands of miles away from where the object was found, to "rediscover" it.

Professor Barton studied the objects very carefully. He was particularly attracted to the one bronze object with the ancient Hebrew writing on it. Slowly he copied the inscription on a piece of paper. Letter by letter he transcribed it, first looking carefully at the metal object, then writing down the letter he thought it represented. The first letter was certainly a lamed, next a zayin, and so on, until the inscription was completely transcribed: Le-Zechariah Yair (Belonging to Zechariah the son of Yair).

Now he turned it on the other side. Here there were only three letters. P – I – M. Pim. What could Pim be? Professor Barton knew that it sounded familiar but for the moment he could not place it.

What Professor Barton did next, as any scholar would do when he came across an object that seemed important, especially one with an inscription, was to write a description of it and publish it in a scholarly journal. His description was published in an article in the 1903 issue of the *Journal of the American Oriental Society.* The article was entitled "A Unique Hebrew Weight." In the article, Professor Barton reported all the details of its physical description: the weight was made of a brassy bronze; it weighed 7.5 grams; it was 7/8″ long, 5/8″ wide; 1/4″ thick at one end and 5/8″ thick at the other end. One side read "Belonging to Zechariah the son of Yair," and the other, "Pim." Its state of preservation was surprisingly good.

Once the information was published, scholars all over the world had the opportunity to study the data and suggest their own interpretations of its significance.

Years passed before any new information came regarding the Pim weight. Several implausible suggestions were advanced, but none was widely accepted.

In 1907, news came of another weight turning up with the same three letters on one side, but nothing on the other. This time the weight was made of stone. It had been found by the English archeologist, R. A. S. Macalister, digging at Gezer, a biblical site in Palestine. This stone object weighed a little bit less than Barton's, but was close enough to indicate that only time had worn its surface somewhat, thus reducing its weight.

When the information about this new weight was circulated, the report stated that "Pim is another unknown word, and we can only conjecture until we know more about it."

A major breakthrough came when a third specimen was found by an Arab farmer, again near Jerusalem, and turned over to an Italian Jew living in Palestine, Signor Samuel Raffaeli. Raffaeli was thoroughly at home in the Hebrew Bible and from the minute the weight passed into his hands, he did not stop thinking about what the mysterious three-letter word Pim could mean.

One night, while reading the Bible, the answer came to him. He was reading the thirteenth chapter of the First Book of Samuel. This chapter tells the story of the Battle of Michmas, in which King Saul was fighting against the Philistines. The Bible reports that the Israelites could not make any weapons because the Philistines prevented them from having a smith. It also states that in order to sharpen farm instruments, the Israelites had to go to the Philistines. One particular verse in the story — verse twenty-one — had given readers difficulty for centuries. A famous commentary, or explanation, of the Book of Samuel, written by one of the greatest early twentieth-century Bible scholars, Samuel R. Driver, confessed about this verse, "These words are hopelessly corrupt."

The English translations of the Bible likewise admit defeat. The Revised Version of the King James Bible, for example, translates "Yet they had a file for the mattocks, and for the coulters . . ." (farm instruments). This plainly contradicts the above verses which state that the Israelites had to go to the Philistines to sharpen blades. In the margin, the translators admitted that "The Hebrew text is obscure." This was an ancient puzzle which commentators and scholars had been wrestling with for centuries.

Raffaeli had been following all the latest developments in archeology and ever since Barton's article appeared in 1903, he had been thinking of a possible meaning for the word Pim. Now, in 1914, he himself had obtained a sample of the Pim weight.

Reading the verse in Samuel, he came across the word Pim, and the correct interpretation came to him like a flash of light.

No one had ever connected this word with the weight itself. Until Mr. Raffaeli came along, all scholars had been connecting the word Pim with the Hebrew word peh, meaning "mouth" or "edge." They thought that perhaps Pim was a plural form of peh — even though it had never appeared before in that form, and in fact was unlikely.

Suddenly the whole puzzle fell into place. The word Pim simply meant what it said — a weight called Pim. Pim was the name of the measure of the weight, like the English pound or ounce.

In the Israel of King Saul's time, there were no coins as such. People used weights as coins. This Pim weight was the price the Israelites paid for having their farm implements sharpened by the Philistines! Now Raffaeli could translate the verse correctly for the first time in two thousand or more years.

The verse therefore meant, "And the price for sharpening the farm implements was a Pim." As simple as that. And yet until the weight with Pim spelled on it appeared, no one could have even remotely guessed what the verse meant. The original Pim discovered by Professor Barton can be seen today in the Museum of Haverford College, outside Philadelphia.

A year after Raffaeli made his astounding report, scholars all over the world accepted it. It was a natural explanation, and fit perfectly into the context of the passage.

A few months after the new interpretation had been offered, it was pointed out in a scholarly magazine by an English scholar, M. H. Segal (later to become Professor of Bible at the Hebrew University), that he too had come across the same explanation. In September 1914, he reported that a new book of his, a commentary on the Books of Samuel, which was then on the press, had the very same interpretation. Unfortunately, the accident of Raffaeli's prior publication had made him the discoverer of the meaning of Pim, but actually the two scholars, Segal and Raffaeli, should be credited with the find.

The first translation of the Bible to embody the discovery by Segal and Raffaeli was in 1917, when the Jewish Publication Society of America published their English version of the Bible in Philadelphia. From that time on, most widely accepted translations have carried the revised wording.

Now that the Pim weight has clarified the difficult verse, we can understand much more of the problem discussed in that chapter of the Bible. Scholars call the period preceding the influx of the Philistines (around 1200 B.C.) the Bronze Age. That is because weapons and farm tools were made mostly from bronze. The era beginning 1200 B.C. is considered the Iron Age. The Philistines knew the secret of the very complex process of smelting iron from iron ore. And so, at the Battle of Michmas, as the chapter in First Samuel informs us, the Philistines had weapons of the stronger, more durable metal—iron—and the Israelites had none.

The Philistines were extremely clever in not giving away their carefully guarded secret. Because of their cleverness, "There was no smith to be found throughout the land of Israel" (I Samuel 13:19). Thus, even to sharpen their farm implements, the Israelites had to go to the Philistine cities and pay an extremely high price for this service. The Philistines operated a successful monopoly on iron implements, charging the Israelites the apparently exorbitant price of a Pim for sharpening their farm tools.

What size weight was a Pim? How much was it worth in ancient times?

The basic unit of weight in Bible days was the shekel. This can be compared to the basic unit of weight in America, the pound. All American weights of relatively small size are either a fraction or a multiple of the basic pound unit: a quarter pound, a half pound, two pounds, ten pounds, etcetera.

It was the same with the shekel. There were fractions and multiples of shekels. The Pim was a fraction of a shekel—probably two-thirds of a shekel. Other fractions of a shekel are mentioned in the Bible: a quarter of a shekel is called a Reba (I Samuel 9:8); a third of a shekel is called a Shalish, and a half of a shekel is called a Bekah (Exodus 38:26).

Now we come to the last problem in our mystery. How do words in the Bible become forgotten?

Actually, this is asking the question in reverse. Considering the age of the books of the Bible—an age varying from two to four thousand years old (depending on the individual book)—we should really ask, "How do the meanings of ancient words remain in the memory of men generation after generation?"

To simplify a very complex matter, the answer is this: As long as a people continues to speak a language in which a book is written, the meanings of the words are retained through daily conversation, and through the written word in letters, documents, etcetera. However, even then new words and new forms of language and expression are introduced, making it necessary for certain words which are no longer in use to be explained from father to son and from teacher to pupil.

When a language passes out of everyday use, as Hebrew did about two thousand years ago (after the loss of Jewish independence in the year A.D. 70), means must be found to retain the understanding of the language if people want to be able to read the books written in that language as it was spoken. For this purpose we have dictionaries, some of which give the meanings of words of a language no longer in use. We also have commentaries, which explain the shades of meanings of words no longer clearly understood due to lack of use. We also have translations of books which help to define words of lost languages. For example, we have translations of the Bible in other ancient languages such as Greek, Latin and Aramaic. (A Semitic language, like Hebrew, Aramaic was the spoken tongue of Jesus.)

By using all of these tools—dictionaries, commentaries, translations of books—a scholar can usually uncover the original meaning of a sentence or paragraph in ancient languages such as Hebrew or Greek. Every once in a while, though, a word comes up which fell out of common use and was totally forgotten even before it could be set down. In a case like that, consulting these aids is of no help. For the same word, a dictionary may give many different meanings. When this happens one can assume that even in ancient times the word was no longer understood and the translator merely guessed to fill in the blank.

When such a problem arises there are still a few ways, developed only in the last century, to reach into the deep recesses of the past and ferret out the meaning of a forgotten word. One of these is archeology.

It is a rare occasion, however, when we find some weight or other object from ancient times which has its name written on it. The miraculous rescue of the word Pim was such a rare occasion. Not only was a weight found with an ancient Hebrew inscription, but it was a word which was forgotten for thousands of years, and which, once rediscovered, helped scholars illuminate the meaning of a verse, and therefore of an entire historical episode in the Bible. Such occasions are much too rare for the pleasure of the archeologist, but they are becoming more frequent as the science of archeology progresses.

7

THE BLACK OBELISK OF SHALMANESER III:
A Non-Biblical View of a Biblical Event

The middle of the last century saw the opening of an era of great archeological discoveries, as one by one the hidden treasures of ancient Assyria and Babylonia were brought to light from under the dust of centuries. The forerunner of the pioneer archeologists was Claudius James Rich (1787–1820), who in his spare time as a British consular official at Baghdad, explored certain huge mounds in the deserts of the biblical region of Mesopotamia. His memoirs, *Memoir on the Ruins of Babylon,* with an account of these explorations, together with sketches and plans for excavations he had been unable to carry out, eventually came into the hands of Paul Émile Botta, an agent of the government of France. In the year 1843, Botta began excavations at Khorsabad, a village not far from Mosul, the capital of Iraq. In a remarkably short time he uncovered a palace that had been built by the order of the Assyrian King Sargon

II, in the eighth century B.C. Many of the sculptured reliefs, cuneiform tablets, and other objects he unearthed on the site are now among the treasures of the Louvre in Paris.

On the heels of these discoveries came those of another pioneer in Assyrian archeology, Sir Austen Henry Layard. Born in Paris of English parents in 1817, he traveled widely as a child. Adventure and exploration seem to have been in his blood; his imagination was fired by reading everything he could that had to do with Asia Minor, from the *Arabian Nights* to the memoirs of Claudius Rich. By the time Botta began the work of unearthing the palace of Sargon, Layard himself had already visited the same region. A restless and resourceful young man, he had developed a genuine love for the people of the Middle East. He made friends with them easily, and although he was repeatedly robbed, once held as a slave by Bedouins and plagued by illness, his enthusiasm for them was undiminished.

He met Botta at Mosul. Eager to begin excavations of his own, he was confronted by the problem of persuading men of means to finance the project. He made sketches of Botta's discoveries at Khorsabad and sent them to London, hinting broadly that given the opportunity—and the funds—he could do for England what Botta had done for France.

The British ambassador to Constantinople was sufficiently impressed to provide Layard with a small sum out of his own pocket. Eventually the British Museum gave him its backing. But the typical stipulation in those days was to obtain "the greatest possible number of well-preserved objects of art at the least possible outlay of time and

Austen Henry Layard drawing at the site of Khorsabad

The Black Obelisk of Shalmaneser III

money." At a time when archeology had kindled the imagination of relatively few, men like Layard had to shift as best they could.

The limitations imposed upon him are evident from his repeated complaints. He wrote, "As the means at my disposal did not warrant an outlay in making more experiments without the promise of the discovery of something to carry away, I felt myself compelled, much against my inclination, to abandon the excavations in this part of the mound." Or again: "The smallness of the sum placed at my disposal compelled me to follow the same plan in the excavations that I had hitherto adopted — viz. to dig trenches along the sides of the chambers, and to expose the whole of the slabs, without recovering the earth from the centre. Thus, few of the chambers were fully explored and many small objects of great interest may have been left undiscovered. As I was directed to bury the building with earth after I had explored it, to avoid unnecessary expense I filled up the chambers with the rubbish taken from those subsequently uncovered, having first examined the walls, copied the inscriptions, and drawn the sculptures."

Nor was the problem of finances the only one that beset archeologists in those days. The rivalries between sponsoring governments made it advisable to move with caution, even secrecy. Iraq was then under Turkish rule, and the provincial governors were often greedy, vengeful and cunning, with no qualms about resorting to bloodshed as a means of intimidating natives and foreign visitors alike. Layard wrote that the pasha at Mosul "was accustomed to give instructions to those who were sent to collect money in three words — 'Go, destroy, eat.' " The natives retaliated with robbery, looting and arson. Their superstitions, and the frequent invocation of the laws of the Koran, added to

Layard's difficulties. The workmen he hired were often fearful of the genii (spirits) that might arise and avenge themselves for the disturbance of their three-thousand-year sleep.

Nevertheless, Layard was remarkably fortunate. At Nimrud, a site not far from Mosul which he chose for his first excavations, he began on the very first day to make rich finds. Trench after trench disclosed palace walls adorned with alabaster slabs covered with cuneiform inscriptions, or carved reliefs depicting scenes of hunting, war and religious ceremonies—an astonishing portrayal of daily life in ancient times. Today they are among the Assyrian treasures on view in the halls of the British Museum. Among them none has greater fascination than the monument known as the Black Obelisk.

The story of the discovery of the Black Obelisk is an exciting one. On a day in December 1846, after a trench fifty feet long had produced nothing of great interest, Layard was about to move on. Then he decided to devote one more day to it, and ordered the workmen to go on digging. He was already on his way to Mosul to attend to some business when an Arab from the excavation caught up with him, breathless with the news that the men had uncovered the edge of a great black stone. Layard rushed back, in time to watch its unearthing.

As he described it: "Although its shape was that of an obelisk, yet it was flat on the top. It was sculptured on the four sides; there were in all twenty small bas-reliefs, and above, below, and between them was carved an inscription of two hundred ten lines in length. The whole was in the best preservation; scarcely a character of the inscription was wanting; the figures were as sharp and well defined as if they had been carved but a few days before. The king is twice represented followed by his attendants; a prisoner is at his feet, and his vizier and eunuchs are introducing men leading various animals, and carrying vases and other objects of tribute on their shoulders, or in their hands. The animals are the elephant, the rhinoceros, the Bactrian or two-humped camel, the wild bull, the lion, the stag, and various kinds of monkeys."

Who was the king? Who was the prisoner? Layard little suspected the great significance of the answers to these questions.

The king was Shalmaneser III (858–824 B.C.). He is not mentioned in the Bible, although there are many colorful stories in the Bible about his prisoner, King Jehu of Israel (842–814 B.C.). The apparent humiliating defeat as described on the obelisk is also not mentioned in the Scriptures. From another inscription by Shalmaneser III (discovered about a decade later) we learn the details of what may have happened.

In the sixth year of his reign (853 B.C.), Shalmaneser III left Nineveh, his capital, for a foray to the west. At Hamath near the Orontes River he was engaged by a union of armies mustered by twelve kings which are listed in detail on the obelisk. Among them was a king from Israel who, according to Shalmaneser, brought along ten thousand foot soldiers. The Assyrians defeated the coalition and the king described his victory on the pillar in some detail:

> . . . I slew fourteen thousand of their soldiers with the sword. . . . I spread their corpses everywhere, filling the entire plain with their widely scattered, fleeing soldiers. . . . The plain was too small to let all their souls descend into the nether

world, the vast field gave out when it came to bury them. With their corpses I spanned the Orontes before there was a bridge.

Despite the savage boastfulness typical of the Assyrian warlords, the battle was not as decisive as it appears. The Assyrians were halted in their invasion of Palestine. But it seems that Israel became a vassal and had to pay tribute to Nineveh. This is evident from the scene depicted on the Black Obelisk. It is surmised that it happened later in Shalmaneser's campaign, in 842 B.C. Over the second row of panels runs a legend that reads:

The tribute of Jehu, son of Omri; I received from him silver, gold, a golden bowl, a golden vase with pointed bottom, golden tumblers, golden buckets, tin, a staff for a king. . . .

The Black Obelisk of Shalmaneser III enjoys the distinction of being the only object that depicts the likeness of an Israelite king. Today it is one of the most prized possessions of the British Museum, and is on display in the Hall of Assyrian Antiquities.

8

THE CLUE FROM THE SUN:
How the Word "Hamman" Came Back to Life

In 1751, long before the science of archeology became an established profession, two young men set out on an archeological expedition. They were Robert Wood and his companion Mr. Dawkins.

At the age of twenty, the two men decided to leave their strictly disciplined lives in London and see the world. Both of them had been interested in ancient history in school. So they decided to pick a faraway city, and explore its ancient remains. Going over the names of cities likely to have many buried treasures, they decided upon the Syrian city of Palmyra, just northeast of ancient Palestine.

Their trip turned out to be very valuable. Their finds were varied and interesting, and included a group of small stone altars.

"These altars have writing on them," said Wood. "I think we should carry them back with us to England. I am certain that a museum will be interested in having them."

"I suppose you are right," answered Dawkins, with an air of uncertainty about him. He wanted to bring back many of the things he had found, but realized that they could take only a limited amount.

Back in London, they approached the curator of the Ashmolean Museum and asked if he was interested in displaying the altars they found in Palmyra, Syria. After carefully examining the altars, the curator noticed the inscriptions. "They look extremely interesting," he said, "I think we will take them." With a sense of pride and accomplishment, the two young adventurers made the formal presentation to the Ashmolean Museum a week later.

Wood and Dawkins found their experience so interesting that they decided to record their itinerary and their findings so that future generations would be able to benefit from their trip. They sat down to work on the book. When they were finally finished, they bound the manuscript, added a title page and sought a publisher. The book was called *The Ruins of Palmyra*.

No one in London would agree to publish the book, so they crossed the English Channel and convinced a publisher in France to sponsor it. The book appeared in Paris in French as *Les Ruins de Palmyre*. The date of publication was 1753.

Just after World War I, Professor Harold Ingholt was teaching Semitic languages at the American University in Beirut, Lebanon. He was particularly interested in the connection of words found in the Hebrew Bible with common, related roots in other Semitic languages. Perhaps, he thought, he would be able to explain the words in the Bible better through knowing languages that belonged to the same family as Hebrew.

One night in his study, he was reading a report on a Princeton University expedition

Wood and Dawkins and their puzzling find

sent to Syria in 1904 and 1909. Among the finds of this expedition Professor Ingholt found two inscriptions in a language called Nabataean. As he peered over these ancient words, he recognized the word "Hamna," similar to the Hebrew word Hamman.

At the very sight of this word he became excited. He called to one of his students. "Do you know what biblical word this Nabataean word is related to?" he asked, to see how well his student was progressing in his studies.

"The Hebrew word Hamman," was the reply.

"Correct," said Ingholt. "Take that concordance and check how many times the word 'Hamman' appears in the Bible." (A concordance is a book with all of the words in the Bible listed alphabetically. Next to each word is a list of the chapters and verses in which the word appears in the Bible.)

"I find eight listings," said the student. "Once in Leviticus, twice in Isaiah, twice in Ezekiel, and three times in Chronicles."

The Professor tested his student once again. "See if you can read all of the verses in which the word 'Hamman' appears, and tell me what it means."

This was a difficult test. A dictionary, or perhaps a Bible translation, might give him the answer, but he had to do it the hard way, on his teacher's orders. He was to read the phrase in the Bible in all eight passages, and figure out for himself what the word meant.

After some deep concentration, Professor Ingholt's student was ready to report his findings.

"Professor," he said hesitantly, "the word Hamman in the Hebrew Bible is obviously an object used in pagan worship. In all eight passages of the Bible either God or His prophets threaten to smash the 'Hamman' to bits, together with other idolatrous cult objects, such as altars, graven and molten images and sacred trees."

"A very good start," said Dr. Ingholt admiringly.

"There is more," retorted the student quickly. "It must be an object fashioned by hand, and placed above the altars of Baalim, the pagan gods."

"An excellent report," said the Professor. "Now check the dictionary and the various Bible translations, and tell me the precise translation."

This seemed to be the easiest part of the work. All it meant was looking up a word. But the young scholar found this second assignment at least as hard as the first. After checking several different dictionaries and translations he still did not have an answer. Instead, he had a dozen different answers.

"Professor," he said in dismay, "every book I turn to seems to yield another translation of Hamman. One says 'images,' another 'idols.' Still a third has 'wooden objects,' and others say 'abominations,' 'sanctuaries,' 'statues' and 'sun-pillars.' I am completely confused."

"Don't be discouraged," said Dr. Ingholt. "You are not the first person to be confused by this word. Actually, no one has understood it for centuries. When the Jews of Alexandria, Egypt, translated the Hebrew Bible into Greek over two thousand years ago, they had no more success than you.

"Since those Jews no longer spoke Hebrew but Greek, they had forgotten what the word meant. They used several different words to translate the same word in different passages. This is the source of the confusion."

"Thank goodness," said the student. "For a moment I thought I was looking at the.

wrong verses when I found all those different translations. Do you really mean, Professor, that for two thousand years no one has understood the word Hamman?"

"Well, not exactly. There have been some educated guesses in the past. The first person to make a sensible translation was a French Rabbi who lived in the eleventh century. He was known as Rashi (after the initials of his names, Rabbi Shelomoh ben Yishaq). Rashi reasoned that the word Hamman must be connected with the Hebrew word for sun, Hammah. There is not too much difference, is there?"

"No, there isn't," replied the young man.

"But his answer was only half correct. It is because of his guess that most modern translations and dictionaries give the meaning of 'sun-image,' or 'sun-pillar.' The most natural thing to surmise was that this was a cult object representing the sun, and by worshipping it, ancient people were worshipping the sun.

"However, in the seventeenth century another suggestion was made by the famous Dutch jurist, Hugo Grotius. Making a careful study of the word in the Bible, he came up with a slightly different translation. He suggested that the word means a pyre, or place where holy fire was brought during pagan worship.

"But now, when I found Hamman written on this ancient inscription discovered by the Princeton Expedition about ten years ago, I called you over to share the excitement. Finally, we may come closer to learning who was really right—Rashi, Grotius, both of them, or neither!"

The Nabataean inscriptions Professor Ingholt studied were only one clue to the solution of the problem of the mysterious and elusive word Hamman. He combed through the libraries for more information leading to the meaning of the unknown word.

Finally, one day he found a book high up on the shelf in the back of the University Library called *Les Ruins de Palmyre* by Wood and Dawkins, published in 1753. In the book he read about three altars they found, with a transcription of the letters found on the altar. He noticed that one of the words read Hamman. This might be the clue to breaking the deadlock.

Ingholt contacted the Ashmolean Museum of London, and had photographs of the altars and the inscription sent to him. On one of the altars was a carving of two men in a standing position, throwing grains of incense on a flaming altar located between them. On the reverse side of the altar was the following inscription: "This Hamman and this altar are offered by Lishamsh and Zebid to the god Shamsh. . . ."

Professor Ingholt examined the photographs of the inscription, and concluded that the Hamman mentioned in it was the altar between the two men, and the scene depicted was the donation ceremony in which Lishamsh and Zebid gave the altar to the gods. Furthermore, the carved image of the altar was exactly the same as the real altar on which it was carved. Thus, the scene and the inscription marked the dedication of the altar.

"Here is the answer," exclaimed the Professor. "Finally we know what Hamman is. It is an incense altar!"

On November 7, 1924, Professor Ingholt gave a lecture on his discovery before the Palestine Oriental Society of Jerusalem. "I have discovered," he declared dramatically, "through the study of a stone altar with an inscription and a carved picture on it, the meaning of the ancient word Hamman. The altar actually has the word Hamman carved on it, with a picture of the Hamman itself.

"The Hamman is therefore an incense altar. It is not a sun-pillar or sun-image as thought by Rashi and others following him. It is a pagan altar on which incense was offered to please the gods with sweet-smelling sacrifices."

A hand was raised in the audience. "Then how do you account for the similarity between the Hebrew words Hammah meaning sun, and 'Hamman' meaning incense altar?"

"The explanation is simple," answered the Professor. "This is the clue given to us by the word Hammah, or sun. The sun gives off heat, and so does the burning incense. This is the answer to the mystery. Both Hebrew words are related to the same root meaning hot."

Over the course of years several examples of these small incense altars with four horns, one on each corner, have been discovered all over Palestine, in places like Megiddo and Shechem.

In 1939, Professor Ingholt was able to marshall all of the accumulated evidence from archeology and Semitic languages, and present a fully explained statement of his theory. He published an article entitled "The Meaning of the Word 'Hamman,'" finally dispelling any doubts still lingering that the Hamman could have anything to do with a sun-image or sun-pillar.

The mystery of the lost word was finally brought to its conclusion, and now the new dictionaries give only one meaning: incense altar. All thanks are due to two adventurous young men from London, and an American scholar who interpreted their discovery over one hundred and fifty years later.

9

THE VAIN PRIME MINISTER:
The Rediscovery of the Shebna Tomb

In May 1870, the famous scholar, Charles Clermont-Ganneau, was sent to Palestine by the Palestine Exploration Fund, a society devoted to unearthing the remnants of biblical civilization in the Holy Land. He was drawn to the village of Silwan, the ancient Siloam, because of the existence there of many ancient tombs.

Silwan lay to the east of Jerusalem, on a rocky slope at the foot of the Mount of Olives. Clermont-Ganneau hoped that one or two of the tombs had escaped the grave robbers who over the centuries had plundered and emptied most of them in that area.

As he was strolling around the neighborhood on the first day of his expedition, he noticed a well-built house whose facade was flush with the street. The house rested on what looked like a warehouse, carved out of the rock. Clermont-Ganneau guessed that the house on top of this rock-cut chamber had been built within the last few decades.

It had modern masonry, in contrast to the smooth rock surface below. The rock had been dressed to a smooth vertical wall in which a doorway and a window, both rectangular in shape, were cut. The chamber was approximately eight feet tall and fifteen feet wide. Above each of the openings, Clermont-Ganneau noticed what seemed to be engravings in recessed panels.

Suspecting that these engravings might be letters, the archeologist took a box from the street and climbed up on it to inspect the wall at close range. The engravings did indeed resemble letters—ancient Hebrew letters. At this point the people of the neighborhood threatened him and forced him to leave.

The following Monday, Clermont-Ganneau made the proper administrative arrangements with the Turkish government and was granted permission to explore. Early Tuesday morning, before the local residents were up, he made his way to the rock-cut chamber. This time he had a stepladder and other necessary equipment. He worked as quietly as possible in order not to disturb the residents of the house. In spite of his efforts, however, they emerged from the house after a few minutes, with angry looks on their faces.

"I am sorry to disturb you so early," the archeologist apologized in Arabic. "I am from a very important European organization that is interested in digging up ancient remains. If I find something of value on your property, it could mean a nice bonus for you."

The man and his wife seemed pleased at this news, and forgave the stranger for awakening them. They dressed and came back out to the street.

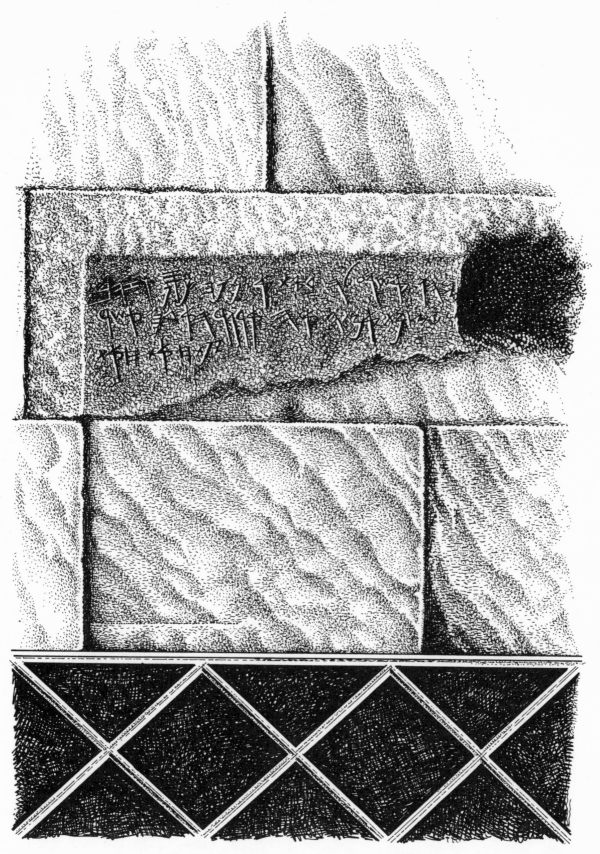

Ancient Hebrew letters above the tomb of Shebna

The Arab's wife saw where the archeologist was working. "I see you are investigating these carvings," she called up to him on the ladder. "Unfortunately, you are some years too late. When we were building our house, the workers had to destroy several lines of this scribbling. They did not know it was important."

Clermont-Ganneau was very disappointed. He had thought that the three line inscription over the door and the one line over the window of the chamber were great finds. Now he learned that this was only part of a larger group of inscriptions which had been destroyed. He was comforted by the fact that he could at least salvage this small remnant.

Upon further examination he concluded that the inscription was indeed ancient Hebrew writing. However, making out the letters seemed to be impossible. They were in very bad shape because of weather and age.

Noticing a few heavy marks on the wall, the archeologist turned back to the street and asked the man, "Were these lines of writing beaten with a hammer?"

"I think they were," was the answer. "In trying to smooth out the surface the builders tried to obliterate these uneven marks. We did not know they were letters."

Again the French scholar felt keen disappointment. He would probably never be able to decipher the letters. But he didn't give up. In addition to taking photographs, he made a plaster cast of the inscription.

To protect the engraved writing itself, Clermont-Ganneau decided to have the entire block of rock with the recessed panels over the door and window cut out and shipped to the British Museum.

He wired the British Consul in Palestine, who in turn contacted the museum. Within one week, he received authorization to spend up to thirty British pounds. This was not much, but it was enough to pay for the cutting, the shipping arrangements and a small indemnity to the owners of the house who, after all, had to replace the panels.

Once the panels were safely in the hands of the curator of the British Museum, Clermont-Ganneau could rest easy. Still, the main job — deciphering the inscription — lay ahead. What did this inscription say? What kind of chamber, or warehouse, did it mark? Was it a sanctuary to ancient pagan gods? Was it a tomb of some important official? Or was it perhaps merely the dwelling of a common peasant of biblical times?

Night after night, the French archeologist sat in his study poring over the photographs and the plaster casts. He recognized that the letters were in the ancient Hebrew script, and he could even pick out and identify an isolated letter here and there.

For thirty years, the scholar pondered the photographs and the plaster casts without success. He simply could not identify enough Hebrew letters to make sense out of them.

In 1899 Clermont-Ganneau published a two-volume work recording many of the discoveries he had made over the past years in Palestine. In describing these two inscriptions he wrote the following:

> *Unfortunately they have both suffered greatly; thus far I have only succeeded in making out a few words, and to this day I have put off publishing the results of my studies, waiting always for an opportunity of making the necessary verification in London from the original stones.*
>
> *The only word which I have been able to read, and that without absolute certainty, is the word* bayit, *house.*

Knowing that Silwan was an area strewn with ancient tombs, he assumed that the words had something to do with a funerary monument. In a footnote at the end of the article, he added that he thought one phrase read "who is over the house." This was the biblical title for the Judean prime minister, the person second to the king, who had charge of the king's house, or palace.

Then he even dared to identify the prime minister: it was Shebna, mentioned in the Book of Kings and in the prophetic Book of Isaiah. But he began to retract this even as he made the suggestion:

"One must be on one's guard," he added, "against these too sanguine illusions."

From 1899 to 1952, almost nothing new was learned about this battered inscription. In 1952, in a book about the city of Jerusalem, one scholar wrote that "The reading of this much damaged inscription, now in the British Museum, is impossible."

All hope seemed to be lost, as a learned opinion five decades later confirmed what Clermont-Ganneau had suspected: the words were too badly worn to yield a translation.

In the following year, 1953, a scholar in the Hebrew University happened to be leafing through Clermont-Ganneau's 1899 report. His curiosity was aroused by something he saw, and he picked up the telephone and called the office of the Foreign Minister.

"Do you think that you could contact the consulate in London, and get some work done for me at the British Museum?" he asked.

"I don't see why not," the official answered.

A short time later, Professor Nahman Avigad had in his possession several photographs of the inscription from London, and in addition a squeeze, or plastic mold, made from the inscription, which enabled him to examine the contents of the writing almost as clearly as if he had the rock with him in Jerusalem.

Avigad had been working with ancient Hebrew letters for decades, and had familiarized himself with every conceivable type of letter formation. Starting on the premise that the words Clermont-Ganneau thought he had mistakenly identified were indeed correct, he proceeded to decipher the whole inscription.

Today, his interpretation of the words and his translation of their meaning are accepted by all scholars. The one word which was so badly blurred that it was impossible to read was the name of the person about whom the inscription was written.

The following is his reading of the inscription. The words in parentheses are supplied from the context, and could not be read in the original.

Line one: *This is (the tomb of) . . . yahu who is over the king's palace. There is no silver and no gold here,*
Line two: *But (his bones) and the bones of his slave-wife with him. Cursed be the man*
Line three: *who opens this.*

Obviously, then, the rock-cut chamber was an ancient burial place. The main question, however, still lay unanswered. Who was the owner of the tomb? Who was the man ". . . yahu"? With only the last few letters of his name, it could have been anyone. Especially since this name ending, "yahu," means "God," and was an extremely popular appendage to ancient Hebrew names.

A second clue, in addition to the name ending, was that the man was prime minister, or "over the king's palace." Thirdly, Avigad was able to date the inscription fairly accurately. He showed that the shape of the Hebrew letters resembled very closely the inscription found in the Siloam Tunnel which dated from the year 700 B.C.

With these three clues—a part of the name, the title and date—Avigad determined that the tomb belonged to a Judean prime minister from the late eighth century whose name ended in "yahu."

Again a snag appeared. There was no record of such a man with a name ending in "yahu."

One day while sitting in his office in the Archeology Department of the Hebrew University, Dr. Avigad heard a knock at the door. It was Major General Yigael Yadin. Yadin looked at the decipherment of the rock engraving and discussed it with Avigad. Finally, the answer came to him.

"This was the tomb of Shebna, Prime Minister of Judah under King Hezekiah," said Yadin excitedly.

"That's impossible," said Avigad. "His name does not end in 'yahu.'"

"That's the point," answered Yadin. "Shebna is not a full name. It is merely a shortened form of the full name, Shebeniah, or in Hebrew, Shebenyahu!"

Quickly the scholars picked up a dictionary of biblical names and found the very name Shebeniah mentioned in the Bible. Shebna met all of the requirements. He held the title "over the king's palace"; he lived around the year 700 B.C., when the inscription on the tomb was written; and his name in its full form ended with "yahu."

Thus, through a combination of ideas, the riddle was solved. The tomb on the hill slopes of Silwan, near ancient Jerusalem, was that of Shebna, the Prime Minister of Judah under King Hezekiah.

But one of the most amazing revelations was yet to come. This very tomb, discovered by Clermont-Ganneau of Paris and identified by Avigad of Jerusalem, is mentioned in the Bible, in the Book of Isaiah. Clermont-Ganneau's wild guess that he had discovered the tomb of Shebna of the Bible turned out to be accurate.

The passage is in Isaiah 22:15–25. The time was in the last decade of the eighth century B.C., when the Southern kingdom of Judah was under Assyrian oppression.

The nation had many political and financial problems, and its leaders should have been worrying about the state. Instead, Shebna built himself a fancy, luxurious tomb in the suburbs of the city, so that after his death his body would be enshrined in a resting place for all to marvel at.

Most tombs in those times were small, underground burial niches. Shebna had an ostentatious one, high on a rock for everyone to see. For this Isaiah predicted his downfall:

> *Thus saith the Lord, God of hosts:*
> *Go, get yourself to that steward, to Shebna*
> *   the Prime Minister:*
> *What have you here, and whom have you here,*
> *   to have cut out a tomb for yourself?*
> *You, who cut your tomb up on high,*
> *   digging yourself an abode in the rock!*
> *Behold, the Lord will shake you like a robe . . .*
> *   to a far away place, where you will die. . . .*

In his prophecy Isaiah foretells removal from office for Shebna, and we read later in the Book of Isaiah that Shebna was indeed demoted from his office and replaced by someone else.

And so, a tomb mentioned in the Prophets is found, and its carved inscription is deciphered and explained over a period of sixty years. The Shebna inscription turned out to be the first Hebrew inscription found from the period of the kings of Judah, and the third longest inscription in existence today. It is the first known text of a Hebrew grave inscription from the pre-Exilic period before 586 B.C. when King Nebuchadnezzar conquered Jerusalem and sent her people to slavery and exile in Babylon.

10

WHO WAS THE LAST KING OF JUDAH?:
The Story of the Jehoiachin Tablets

In 1898, a group of archeologists was sent by the German Oriental Society to investigate the ancient mound believed to be Babylon, glorious city of biblical times. This group, headed by Robert Koldewey, later claimed to have unearthed many important ancient remains, including the Tower of Babel, the Palaces of Nebuchadnezzar and Nabopolassar (kings of ancient Babylonia), and the famous Hanging Gardens, which the Greeks regarded as one of the seven wonders of the world. Even though not all of these finds turned out to be what the excavators thought they were, the expedition was still a very productive one.

One of the most important discoveries was not immediately understood as being of major importance.

At the bottom of a stairwell in an underground chamber, the archeologists found three hundred tablets. Their conjecture, probably correct, was that the tablets fell down there when the upper stories of the building collapsed. The tablets were written in cuneiform characters in the international language of the day, Akkadian. They dated from the sixth century B.C., around the time of the prophet Jeremiah.

These important tablets were brought back to Germany, and the hard-working archeologists continued to excavate the mound of ancient Babylon for fourteen years, until the beginning of World War I. The contents of the tablets were not published until many years later.

In 1928 a related discovery was made by Professor William Foxwell Albright at a mound in Palestine called Tell Beit Mirsim (the biblical city Debir). Albright dug up a broken jar handle, with a seal impression stamped on it. Stamping a seal, or mark of identification, on the handle of a jar was a common practice in ancient times. This important jar handle had the following stamp on it:

BELONGING TO ELIAKIM, STEWARD OF YAUKIN

Albright tried to discover who Yaukin might have been. At that time, the great French biblical scholar, Father L. H. Vincent, was living in Palestine. Albright's dig at Tell Beit Mirsim was not too far from the French Bible School where Vincent was teaching. Luckily, Albright thought of consulting his friend and colleague, who agreed to study the jar handle. The two scholars met again the next day. "Fortunately," declared Father Vincent, "I have been able to come up with a very likely solution to the problem."

"Who is this Yaukin?" asked Albright, impatient to know whether his discovery had any significance.

"On the basis of other Hebrew names I have come across, I would venture to say that this is an abbreviation of a name you know very well, Dr. Albright: Jehoiachin."

Albright did not have to be convinced. He recognized the soundness of this suggestion immediately: "Steward of Yaukin—who would have a steward but a member of royalty? Of course, King Jehoiachin!"

Two years later, a colleague of Albright's found an identical jar handle, and Albright himself found yet another. Now three jar handles were available for study. What did they mean? What new information did they give Bible scholars about the young king of Judah who was taken captive by King Nebuchadnezzar of Babylonia around the time of Jeremiah?

Their real significance became known when, in 1939, the handles were linked to the cuneiform documents found in Babylonia by Robert Koldewey around thirty years before. Dr. Ernst F. Weidner, a German biblical scholar, had studied these tablets in the early 1930's, and in 1939 he published a few of them in a book containing a collection of articles by great scholars from many countries.

One of the names on these tablets was Yaukin and he was called king of Judah. Now there could be no doubt about it. Father Vincent's suggestion was now a confirmed fact. Yaukin *was* a king of Judah, as he and Albright had deduced—none other than King Jehoiachin. This abbreviated form of the name was more commonly used than either of them had suspected.

Who was King Jehoiachin, and what connection could his name have with faraway Babylonia, where the tablets were found? The answer is in the Bible, chapters 24 and 25 of the Second Book of Kings.

The following is the story contained there, in a somewhat embellished and reconstructed form:

At the end of the sixth century B.C., the new power of the day was the rising empire of Chaldea (or Neo-Babylonia as it is sometimes called). This strong empire ruled the ancient East from 626 to 539 B.C. — less than a century, but very important years for Bible history. These years saw the burning of the Temple in Jerusalem, the destruction of the capital itself, and the exile of most of the Jewish community of Judah to Babylonia. The second part of this era, from 586 B.C. on, is known as the "Babylonian Exile."

In the year 626 B.C., the first king of the new Babylonian empire, Nabopolassar, began to spread his wings and conquer the then known world. As part of his plan to bring many nations under his heel, he sent his son Nebuchadnezzar to head off Pharaoh Necho of Egypt, who was on his way north to aid crumbling Assyria, enemy of Babylonia. Nebuchadnezzar defeated Necho at a city in Syria called Carchemish in 605 B.C.

With this victory under his belt, Nebuchadnezzar was anxious to push farther south and win more territory. But that same year he received the news of the death of his father, King Nabopolassar. He hurried back home to Babylon to claim the throne, fearing that someone might attempt to wrest it from the ruling family. He arrived in time to take control of the situation and be crowned king of Babylonia in 605 B.C.

While Nebuchadnezzar was in Babylon, Egypt took advantage of the time to build herself up, and to recover from the defeat at Carchemish. In 601 B.C., there was another battle, and this time both sides suffered heavy losses. The mighty Nebuchadnezzar was in no condition to make new conquests until he repaired his army.

King Jehoiakim (608–598 B.C.), father of Jehoiachin, who had submitted to Nebuchadnezzar without a struggle, thought that this was a good opportunity for him to break the yoke of Babylon from his neck, and he rebelled. This was a tragic error and even his subjects realized it. The meager evidence we have indicates that there was a palace revolt. Jehoiakim's body seems to have been thrown outside the city gates, like the carcass of a donkey, and left to die.

His unfortunate eighteen-year-old son was left holding the tattered reins of power. He became King Jehoiachin in December 598 B.C., and three short months later was faced with the choice of fighting mighty Babylonia or surrendering. Wisely, he chose to surrender, and saved his country from complete destruction. In March 597 B.C., Nebuchadnezzar carried Jehoiachin off to exile as a prisoner. With him went his mother, Nuhushta, his servants, princes, officers, and the elite of Jerusalem's political leadership, totaling some ten thousand people. And as the Bible reports (II Kings 24:14):

None remained, except the poorest sort of the people of the land.

Nebuchadnezzar also took all of the valuable treasures of the Temple—the gold vessels and silver ornaments of Solomon's magnificent House of God.

In place of Jehoiachin, Nebuchadnezzar put a man of his own choice on the throne—the former king's uncle, Zedekiah. Zedekiah remained king for eleven years, until 586 B.C. when Jerusalem and the Temple were finally put to the torch by hungry, destructive Babylonia. The year 586 B.C. marks the beginning of the Babylonian Exile.

Jews in captivity in Babylonia

In that year, the rest of the inhabitants of Judah were marched off to Babylonia. Judah was no more.

All these events have been confirmed by the discovery of the Babylonian Chronicle. This Chronicle consists of documents discovered over the course of the twentieth century, starting in 1907, which give the Babylonian side of the story—the official annals of the Babylonian kings.

The next we hear of Jehoiachin is thirty-seven years after his dethronement, when he is reported released from prison in Babylon by Nebuchadnezzar's successor.

What happened during these thirty-seven years? Archeologists drew a blank until Albright's jar handles and Koldewey's tablets came to light. Thanks to them, new and amazing details have been unearthed about this period of history.

The few but significant tablets whose contents Weidner published in 1939, from Koldewey's larger collection, are records of food rations. Even such a routine piece of evidence tells us a great deal. The rations are sesame oil and grain apportioned by the Babylonian government to certain workers and captives coming from such places as Egypt, Phoenicia, Asia Minor and Persia, and now living in the capital city, Babylon. They deal with the years 595 to 570 B.C. The one with Yaukin's name is dated 592 B.C.:

> ½ *Pi (about 3 gallons) for Yaukin,*
> *king of the land of Yahud;*
>
> *2½ sila (about 3½ pints) for the*
> *five sons of the king. . . .*

Others mentioned in the tablets are mariners, musicians, shipbuilders, craftsmen and even monkey trainers.

What have we learned from these finds? First, although the Bible (II Kings 25:27 ff.) states that the king was in prison when Nebuchadnezzar's son freed him in 562 B.C., he was most likely imprisoned *after* 592 B.C., the date of our tablet. If he received royal rations for himself and his sons he must have had access to his own kitchen, and probably was free to come and go under a casual surveillance of the Babylonian Secret Service. It is not impossible that he tried to take advantage of this freedom to break out and get back to Judah to rebuild his kingdom. An occasion such as this would have had him put behind bars, from whence, in 562 B.C., he was freed.

Second, since he was not imprisoned all those thirty-seven years, as previously thought, he could have been with his family and raised children, which he did. Before these discoveries, it was thought that the sons mentioned in the Bible were born after his release. We now know that five of them were born before 592 B.C., the date of the rations document mentioning them and their guardian, Hananiah.

The most astonishing thing these documents revealed is this: Yaukin, or Jehoiachin, is still called king. "Yaukin, king of the land of Yahud."

How could this be? We know that Nebuchadnezzar placed Zedekiah on the throne. Wasn't he king of Judah now? Were there two kings, one in Judah and one in exile? It is hard to tell, but this may have been the situation. The accepted interpretation is as follows:

Jehoiachin was still officially king of Judah. His captors held him so that the conquered people would behave themselves and be passive prisoners, under threat of causing harm to their king. In other words, Jehoiachin was a hostage. Zedekiah, his uncle, was placed on the throne to handle governmental matters. Actually, he may have been merely a regent or temporary substitute for the king, who the hopeful Judeans expected would soon return to his former glory. A clever move by the Babylonians. This may explain why Zedekiah was such a weak and vacillating ruler.

This contention that Jehoiachin was still the legitimate king is supported by several biblical passages, particularly in the writings of the two major prophets of these troubled days, Jeremiah and Ezekiel.

Hananiah, the son of Azzur of Gibeon, quoted God as saying (Jeremiah, chapter 28):

> *Thus speaketh the Lord of hosts, the God of Israel, saying: I have broken the yoke of the king of Babylon. Within two full years will I bring back into this place all the vessels of the Lord's house, that Nebuchadnezzar king of Babylon took from this place and carried to Babylon; and I will bring back to this place Jehoiachin, king of Judah with all the captives of Judah that went to Babylon.*

Evidently Hananiah was the spokesman for many Jerusalemites who still believed that their real king would soon return and lead them.

From chapter 29 of Jeremiah, we see that the Jews of Judea as well as those carried into captivity with Jehoiachin looked to the eighteen-year-old monarch as their king. Jeremiah had to preach to the Babylonian Jews to strike roots in their new country because the exile would not end for a long time. It follows, then, that most of the people expected a speedy return to their homeland, with their king restored to his throne.

We see from the Book of Ezekiel that the people still believed that Jehoiachin was their king. They dated events not from the reign of the new king, Zedekiah, but from the exile of the *true* king, Jehoiachin.

Furthermore, in the New Testament the line of the Messiah is traced from the early history of Israel through all of their kings to Jehoiachin, and not Zedekiah.

Added to this evidence are the jar handles discovered by Albright. On them are written, "Belonging to Eliakim, steward of Yaukin."

According to Albright, a man named Eliakim had been appointed, after Jehoiachin's exile, as steward, or guardian, of the exiled king's royal property. Underlying this appointment is the assumption that the king is still king, and that he will eventually return and reclaim his possessions. Otherwise, if Jehoiachin were expected to die in captivity and never return, his crown property would have been turned over to his successor. Obviously it was felt that he had no successor because he was still king. In such circumstances Zedekiah could hardly appropriate this royal property.

Among Albright's students, which include many of the great archeologists and Bible scholars of our day, the above view is patently accepted. However, other scholars have pointed out that nowhere in the Bible is Zedekiah mentioned as regent. He is called *king*. In addition, Zedekiah had a close family tie to the throne since he was also the son of a king of Judah, Josiah, and he was older than Jehoiachin.

Whoever is right, we can at least say that there are two kings who rival for position of last king of Judah—one in Judah, and one in exile in Babylonia. Who was really king? We may never know for sure, but archeology has at least led us much closer to the truth.

11

FROM THE KING OF PERSIA TO THE SHAH OF IRAN:
The Story of the Cyrus Cylinder

In 1966, the government of Israel appointed a special committee known as the Special Celebration Committee for King Cyrus. In the same year the modern king of Iran was formally crowned. Together with his coronation, he celebrated the two thousand five hundredth anniversary of the founding of the Persian Empire by Cyrus the Great.

What possible connection could there be between the modern Jewish state and the ancient king of Persia, Cyrus the Great? Why did Israel go to such effort to be an important part of those celebrating this momentous occasion?

The answer lies on a broken terra-cotta cylinder, found by an archeologist in 1879 and in the fact that King Cyrus in 539 B.C. freed the Jews living in Babylonian exile and permitted them to return to their own land, the land of Israel. Were it not for Cyrus,

The tomb of King Cyrus

they might never have returned in 538 B.C., and thus could not possibly have returned again in 1948.

The new king of Iran stands proudly in the tradition of his ancestor. He, too, has a warm and cordial relationship with Israel even though all the other Moslem nations of the Middle East are hostile to the new Jewish nation.

But this should not surprise us. Because King Cyrus, the founder of the empire of Persia, was in his day a pioneer, and a man of peace and goodwill.

To a Babylonian-born British subject named Hormuzd Rassam goes the credit for the discovery of the broken terra-cotta cylinder which is the central object of attention in this story. His amazing discovery was made in 1879. But to tell the full story we must go back to 1847.

On June 24, 1847, British archeologist Sir Austen Henry Layard, after digging at the sites of ancient Babylon and Nineveh, left the modern city of Mosul with an ambitious young man who had served him faithfully, Hormuzd Rassam.

"Your work has been outstanding," Layard told the young man. "The fact that you were born in Mosul, and speak the native dialect, has been of immeasurable help to me. Now, however, both of us have suffered from malaria and are weak. It is good that we pause for a while. We shall continue again later."

"Whatever you say, Sir," answered the young man. "I am at your service."

Layard and Rassam returned to the ancient Babylonian and Assyrian ruins in October 1849, and remained until March of the following year. In these short campaigns they made phenomenal discoveries, including the famous library of the Assyrian king Ashurbanipal, grandson of Sennacherib.

A few years later, Layard found that he had enough confidence in Rassam to turn the entire project over to his supervision. Besides, he wanted to take time to write up reports on his finds. Rassam returned to the Fertile Crescent on his own in 1853. He found even more precious tablets from the time of Ashurbanipal. By the time his funds ran out, he was able to report to his sponsor, the British Museum:

"I have found over twenty-five thousand tablets. This, together with what Layard and I found within the past decade, will put the modern study of Mesopotamian language and literature on a firm footing."

He was right. These discoveries are the foundation of the study of the entire Babylonian-Assyrian culture of prebiblical times.

Twenty years later Rassam's archeological discoveries again hit the British newspapers. In 1876, the British Museum's Board of Trustees found that their budget was large enough to include the organization of an archeological expedition. An approach was made to Rassam, who willingly agreed to take charge of the expedition. Before World War I, Turkey ruled the Middle East, and the authorities at Constantinople had to give their permission for any such work. This was easily arranged, since Rassam's old friend and former teacher, Layard, was now the Special Representative of Great Britain at Constantinople. Digging concessions were arranged for without delay.

The first of four annual expeditions began in January 1878. Many problems and difficulties beset the pioneer excavator. Rassam reported some of these obstacles in a letter he wrote home shortly after arrival near ancient Babylon.

"Unfortunately, I am not the first to dig here. Others, many others, have preceded me. But they were not excavators. They were local Arabs. They were not looking for remnants of ancient Babylon, even though that is what they found. They were hunting merely for building materials for their homes in the small towns and villages on both sides of the Euphrates. Scores of these homes, up and down the river, are constructed from materials dug out of the ruins of Babylon and other ancient cities.

"But, unfortunately, that is not all," he continued. "Many of these brick-diggers had a clever bone in their heads. They could recognize antiquities when they saw them, and sold them to enterprising dealers who wanted to make fast profits, regardless of the consequences."

One of the worst things that Rassam described was the way some of the natives capitalized on their finds.

"In most cases, the natives break or lose what they find. Often they try to make a bargain by breaking the inscription or other object into fragments, and dividing it among their customers. This is indeed a terrible tragedy."

Rassam was able to devise a clever plan to prevent the local brick-diggers from interfering with his labors. He hired them to be his own diggers and excavators. He offered them, in addition to their wages, the opportunity to keep any bricks they found for themselves, as long as all monuments, inscriptive tablets and other precious articles of antiquity would be turned over to him. He, in turn, sent them, carefully crated, to the British Museum.

The excavator trained the workers to dig carefully. They had been used to clumsy methods in extracting the delicate artifacts from the soil. The objects, he instructed them, were fragile, and had to be treated with care. What a tragedy it was, he explained, that an object of inestimable worth might sit quietly under the soil for thousands of years, only to be carelessly smashed at the hands of an irresponsible digger.

When Rassam's expedition formally began, there were two modern villages on the site of ancient Babylon. In one of these, the town of Jimjima, he made his home. Among the ruins of Jimjima, Rassam discovered a small, broken, terra-cotta cylinder with writing on it. Among the many important finds he made in 1879, this was the one which to this day has significance in biblical history.

At first, Rassam was not sure of its importance. He gave it to Sir Henry Creswicke Rawlinson, an expert cuneiform translator. Rawlinson's translation made headlines around the world.[1]

The broken cylinder contained the official record of the taking of Babylon by Cyrus the Great, in 539 B.C. The account paralleled the biblical story in the Book of Ezra and elsewhere, and added some important details.

Cyrus became the king of a small province which paid tribute to the Median Empire in 559 B.C. Five years later, he rebelled against the Median Empire, and became its king. After other conquests, he turned his attention to Babylon. The event is described, in part, in Daniel, chapters 4–5.

Babylon was ripe for conquest. In fact, the people were so disgusted with their ruler, King Nabonidus, that they did not even put up a fight. They welcomed Cyrus with open arms. According to the official record in the cylinder the Babylonians "bowed to Cyrus and kissed his feet. They were glad that he was king. Their faces lit up."

[1] "Secret Codes and Forgotten Languages," *Worlds Lost and Found,* Azriel Eisenberg and Dov Peretz Elkins (Abelard-Schuman, New York, 1964).

Terra-cotta cylinder of King Cyrus

Nabonidus had neglected the worship of the cherished gods of Babylon, Bel, Nebo and Marduk. Cyrus set himself up as a liberator, rather than a conqueror. He declared that none other than Marduk chose him to take over the kingdom. "Marduk scoured all the lands for a friend, seeking for the upright prince whom it would have to take his hand. He called Cyrus. . . . Marduk the great lord, compassionate to his people, looked with gladness on his good deeds and his upright intentions. Marduk put an end to the power of Nabonidus the king who did not show him reverence. . . ."

Cyrus describes his just policy in the cylinder. "I did not allow any to terrorize the land. . . . I kept in view the needs of Babylon and all its sanctuaries to promote their well being. I lifted their yoke. Their dwellings I restored. I put an end to their misfortunes."

Bible students remember Cyrus for the action he took in the first year of his reign. Since the kingdom of Judah had been conquered by Babylonia in 586 B.C., and the people exiled to the land of the victors, both the Jews and the land of Judah now came under the rule of Cyrus.

In 538 B.C., at the very inception of his rule, Cyrus created a policy of treating all captured nations with justice, and allowed them to worship their own gods. Prior to Cyrus all conquerors had murdered or exiled their victims, destroying the conquered cities.

Cyrus' humane treatment of the exiled Jews is described accurately in Ezra, chapter 1.

In the first year of Cyrus king of Persia, the Lord stirred up the spirit of Cyrus to make a proclamation throughout his kingdom, saying: "Thus says Cyrus, king of Persia, the Lord, God of heaven, has given me all the kingdoms of the earth, and has charged me to build him a house at Jerusalem, which is in Judah. Who ever there is among you of all His people, may His God be with him, let him go up to Jerusalem, and rebuild the house of the Lord, the God of Israel."

Cyrus treated the Jews with justice and kindness. He returned the exiled people to their homeland, and helped them rebuild the Temple. He gave them back the sacred vessels which had been taken to Babylon.

In the Cyrus cylinder, the great king pictured himself as being sent by Marduk. In the Bible, he declares that the God of Israel stirred up his spirit. The meaning is the same. He helped each nation worship the way it pleased. His policy favored freedom of religion, and national development. He will ever be remembered as a humanitarian, who pictured himself as a man of destiny. His support for the return to Zion by the battered and exiled nation of Judah enabled the poet to sing this song (Psalm 126):

> *When the Lord restored the fortunes of Zion*
> *we were like dreamers.*
> *Then our mouth was filled with laughter,*
> *and our tongue with shouts of joy;*

The broken clay cylinder, the Cyrus cylinder, with this famous story written on it, now lies in the British Museum's Babylonian and Assyrian Room.

12

THE MYSTIFYING DURA SYNAGOGUE MURALS:

"Images" in the Synagogue

One of the aftermaths of World War I was the need to police wandering Arab tribes in Mesopotamia who robbed caravans and pillaged the countryside. One such police patrol was commanded by Captain Murphy, an officer of a British battalion of sepoys, or native troops, from India. He bivouacked at a ruined site which, because of the wadi and river which surrounded it on three sides, appeared to be easily defensible. Indeed it looked as if long ago it had been a fortress.

While digging in and setting up the camp site, his men discovered a large hall. To their surprise, they saw brightly colored frescoes, or paintings, of men and objects on the walls. They reported their find immediately to Captain Murphy who in turn reported his discovery, accompanied by rough sketches of the frescoes, to Miss Gertrude Bell, a prominent archeologist who was stationed in Baghdad. Fortunately Professor James H.

Breasted, a leading American Egyptologist, was visiting with her and she persuaded him to go to Dura and investigate the site. He identified the place as the ancient Dura-Europus.

Soon political events and military developments interposed and the territory was ceded to France as part of its mandate of Syria. But before the British withdrew, Breasted did a quick dig and photographed some of the larger murals. Some ten years later another American archeologist who took part in excavating Dura wrote of Breasted's brief excavation, that "it was archeology's biggest single day's work."

Breasted lectured on his discovery, and his lectures and notes led to one of the major archeological excavations of the twentieth century, by a joint team from Yale University and the French Academy of Inscriptions and Belles-Lettres. The site chosen by Yale Professor Michael Rostovtzeff, one of the leaders of the expedition, was a vast mound of sand. The choice turned out to be a fortunate one. On a day in November 1932, eleven years after the chance find that started it all, five young people had the thrill of seeing a painted wall uncovered, in an excellent state of preservation, in the sands where they had been digging. As the excavation proceeded, it disclosed the remains of an entire city block, the ruins of ancient Dura-Europus.

Never an important center in itself, Dura, originally founded about 300 B.C., lay on the trade route between Baghdad to the east and Damascus to the west. It had probably been built as part of a chain of fortresses under the Seleucids, the Syrian-Greek rulers who followed Alexander the Great. In the year A.D. 165, it had been conquered by the Romans. Not quite a century later, in A.D. 256, the Sassanid rulers of Persia laid siege to Dura. To strengthen the fortifications against the battering of this enemy from the east, the Roman defenders heaped up an embankment of sand and clay between the wall and the houses just behind it.

This furnished the answer to two questions that at first puzzled the excavators: first, why the walls and the houses near them were so well preserved; and second, whether the layer of sand and clay that was responsible for their preservation was a natural accumulation, the work of desert winds and drifting sands, or man-made. The discovery of certain inscriptions and coins associated with known historical figures made it possible to date the events that had taken place.

What especially thrilled the excavators, and what has continued to excite the wonder of archeologists ever since, was a building that had clearly been a synagogue, one quite unlike any previously discovered. With a capacity of about sixty-five persons, it was larger than the Christian house of worship that stood nearby. The synagogue was so well preserved that the holes in the floor that had once held the legs of lampstands and reading desks in place were still plainly to be seen.

But what made the synagogue remarkable was its mural decorations. About half of these, a total of thirty panels in color, had been preserved. They were arranged in four horizontal rows, with their focus on the west wall, where the Torah shrine was located. The lowest row formed a frieze composed of animals, masks and geometric designs. The three upper rows depicted biblical scenes. The figures, arranged in no particular order, included the patriarchs—Abraham, Isaac and Jacob; the twelve sons of Jacob; the two sons of Joseph; Moses, Aaron and Miriam; the prophets Samuel, Elijah and Ezekiel; the kings Saul, David and Solomon; Queen Esther, Ahasuerus, Mordecai and

The mystifying murals in the synagogue at Dura

Haman. Names, titles and comments were inscribed on the paintings in Aramaic and Greek. Among the names were those of several men who were evidently a committee of leaders responsible for the building of the synagogue.

From an inscription found on the building, archeologists are agreed that it and the murals must date to around A.D. 244–245. From coins discovered as the excavation of Dura progressed, it likewise became clear that an earlier synagogue had been in existence, built probably at some time between A.D. 165 and 200. Among the coins found in the ruins were some struck as long ago as the reign of the Maccabean king John Hyrcanus (175–104 B.C.), and other later coins dating to the reign of the Herods. It is known that in 130 B.C. John Hyrcanus led a Judean army eastward to help the Seleucid ruler, Antiochus VII, against the growing power of the Persians. From all this it is safe to assume that some Jews were already living in Dura before the great dispersion that followed the destruction of the Temple at Jerusalem in A.D. 70.

The earlier synagogue was a modest building on an obscure street. It seems to have served also as a dwelling, and to have provided a room where Jewish wayfarers might be lodged. It had a special repository for the Torah and another for the sacred scrolls. Unlike the synagogue known to have existed in Galilee during the same period, in this early building the space where the women sat was not in a gallery above the main hall, but in a separate room alongside it. Nor did the earlier synagogue contain pictorial decorations. Whether this was because of the conservatism of those early Jewish inhabitants of Dura, or simply because they lacked the means, is a question that may never be answered.

Under the Romans, Dura was essentially a military base, and whatever commerce there may have been was dependent on the Roman garrison. Undoubtedly the Jewish community profited from it just as their neighbors did. And no doubt the Jews were in contact with their brethren elsewhere — both with Jerusalem to the southwest and with the rapidly growing centers of Jewish learning in Babylon, Sura and Nehardea. That the community grew in numbers and affluence is evident from the renovation and rebuilding of the synagogue. But the most impressive evidence is in the decoration of the third century synagogue with splendid and costly frescoes.

The most challenging and intriguing question about the Dura murals is that they should have been permitted at all. According to the second of the Ten Commandments, as set forth in Exodus 20:4, "Thou shalt not make unto thee a graven image, nor any manner of likeness, of any thing that is in heaven above, or that is in the earth beneath, or that is in the water under the earth." This commandment would seem clearly to prohibit Jews from producing either paintings or sculpture.

The same repugnance is expressed in the writings of the first-century Jewish historian, Flavius Josephus. In his *Antiquities* (Book XVII), he tells of a group of heroic young men who sacrificed their lives in order to pull down the eagle placed by Herod above the entrance to the Temple at Jerusalem. In another passage (*Antiquities,* XVIII) he tells of the rioting of the Jews when Pontius Pilate's legions entered Jerusalem bearing military standards on which the image of the Roman emperor appeared.

But as the Jewish people came into increasingly close contact with the civilizations of Greece, Rome and Persia, a certain amount of relaxation and adaptation was perhaps inevitable. The shift away from the strict prohibition of images toward a concern with other matters of ethics is reflected in the Talmud.

At the end of the first or the beginning of the second century, the attitude of Jews toward "graven images" seems to have changed openly. The Patriarch Rabban Gamaliel visited the baths of Aphrodite at Acco. When asked how he could permit himself to go into a house adorned with the statue of Aphrodite, he dismissed the implied criticism by saying, "I did not come into her premises; she came into mine"; that is, the statue was merely brought to decorate the baths, another matter entirely from building a temple to honor the goddess.

In the third century, the illustrious Rabbah of Babylonia ruled that no objection need be made to a statue set up as an adornment in a large city, but that statues were to be prohibited in villages and rural hamlets where they might become objects of worship by the peasant populace. We also read in the Talmud that certain rabbis did not hinder the decoration of synagogues with wall paintings and mosaic floors. This relaxed attitude was more and more in evidence during the third and the early part of the fourth century.

These incidents and rulings indicate a growing sophistication among Jews concerning the nature of art. Where there was any suspicion that statues might serve as bait to idol worship or the deification of human beings, they were prohibited. Likewise, where statues were used for political ends—such as an assertion that supreme loyalty was due to the Roman emperor—they were opposed. On the other hand, it is clear from the account of two Babylonian rabbis in the third century, who prayed freely in synagogues where the statue of a king had been installed, that the second commandment was not always literally observed. This is in keeping with the statement in the Jerusalem Talmud that "at the time of Rabbi Jochanan"—that is, in the third century—"Jews began to have paintings on the wall and the rabbis did not hinder them from doing so." Thus it is reasonable to believe that the community at Dura in no way went counter to Jewish tradition, but rather reflected a growing sense of freedom and accommodation.

The precise interpretation of the paintings at Dura is still a matter of debate among scholars. In general, it would appear that they were designed to portray the persons and events concerned with the Covenant between God and his people Israel, and to foster reverence for the traditions of the Jews. The faces of the biblical heroes are stylized, although their costumes have a certain individuality. The depiction of animals as ceremonial objects is realistic. It appears that many of the paintings are influenced by the postbiblical commentaries, such as the Midrash, in which the rabbis supplied explanations, moralized or merely fanciful, in order to admonish and instruct their people. Who the artists were, and whether there were several or only one, are matters still to be settled.

From the names inscribed on the walls it would appear that the Jewish community of Dura included both descendants of early settlers and a number of proselytes, and that in turn the community had become to some extent Hellenized, or assimilated into the predominantly Greek culture of that time and region. What gives the murals their special interest is that they are evidence of the development of Jewish pictorial art at an early date. They may be regarded as a forerunner of Christian Byzantine art, out of which the ikons of later centuries developed, and thus shed light on the relation between the art of Judaism and Christianity.

Whether the Dura synagogue murals were unique, or whether there were others of the same kind, is a question that remains to be answered. There may have been many synagogues of the same kind, which were destroyed long ago or obliterated by sun, rain and sand-laden winds. Without any clues, it is impossible to settle the intriguing question of whether the Dura artists were pioneers, or whether they worked in a style that was already established, from models that existed elsewhere.

One of the many unanswered questions about the Dura synagogue is raised by certain inscriptions that are in neither Aramaic nor Greek, but rather the ancient form of Persian known as Pahlavi. These do not, like the other inscriptions, refer to the paintings or to the building of the synagogue, but consist of pious invocations and thanksgivings. Some authorities maintain that the Pahlavi inscriptions are nothing more than casual scribblings, not unlike those found on the walls of public monuments today. Others believe they are connected with the visit of certain Persians to Dura, perhaps (according to one calculation) in A.D. 253. Who were these visitors? Were they Persian Jews, or representatives of the Sassanid dynasty? What was the purpose of their visit? All this remains a mystery. The inscriptions in Pahlavi were evidently executed over a period of six months or longer. Most of them are on the panel depicting Mordecai and Esther. Was this accidental, or was there a distinct purpose behind it? No one knows; but it suggests the possibility that the Dura Jews may have wished to call the attention of their visitors, whoever they were, to a period in Persian history when their own forebears had been favored and protected.

At any rate, we know that not many years after that presumed visit, Dura was swiftly and suddenly destroyed. The buttressing of the walls — buttressing that was to preserve the murals of the synagogue for posterity—was futile against the onslaught of the Persian invaders. It is interesting to note that the eyes of some of the painted figures appear to have been gouged out. Was this the work of Roman soldiers defending the city, or of the Persians who captured it? Was it an act of fanaticism, or merely vandalism? We may never know.

Nor do we know the fate of the Jewish community that was brought to an end by the destruction of the city of Dura. There is some evidence that the members of the community had removed the Ark of the Torah, the scrolls, the lampstands and possibly even the benches before they fled the city. Did they find their way eastward to Babylon, or westward to Judea? Or were they simply swallowed up among the rest of the refugees who swarmed from the doomed fortress?

Whatever their fate, the murals they left behind are today among the prized treasures of the Syrian National Museum at Damascus, and they are the subject of a scholarly volume, the first in a projected series of three, by Dr. Erwin R. Goodenough, Professor of Religion at Yale University. Goodenough says of the discovery that it "had quite as radical implications for our knowledge of Judaism as the Dead Sea scrolls, if not far deeper," and he has dedicated the volume "to the memory of Samuel the Presbyter, Samuel son of Sapharah, Abram the Treasurer, Joseph son of Abba Uzzi, Silas, Salmanes the Proselyte, who built the synagogue at Dura and disclosed new-old depths in Judaism." These are the men whose names were inscribed on the walls of the Dura synagogue, whose accidental discovery is a rich contribution toward the reconstruction of Jewish life in the ancient world.

13

THE SAMARITANS AND THE DALIYEH PAPYRI:
Light on a 2700 Year Old Jewish Sect

Ever since 1947, when the Bedouin tribe of the Ta'amireh discovered the priceless Dead Sea Scrolls in the Qumran caves of Judea, there have been indefatigable explorations of the desolate region around the Dead Sea, in the hope of finding more treasures of the past. Fifteen years after the first discovery, came the startling news of another find. As reported by Dr. Frank Moore Cross, Jr., in *The Biblical Archeologist* (December 1963), in April 1962 Dr. Paul W. Lapp, then Director of the American Schools of Oriental Research in Jerusalem, learned that Père Roland de Vaux of the French Biblical Archeology School received a newly found papyrus fragment from the Palestine Archeological Museum.

Lapp concluded that it was an official document and that it could be dated to 375 B.C. Negotiations for purchase of the papyri from the Ta'amireh Bedouin tribe were

---

consummated in November 1962. The lot, including coins, sealing, etcetera, was purchased by the American School. Cross, who became its director, was given the right of publication. Lapp undertook to excavate further in the Wadi el-Daliyeh caves where the papyri had been found.

The Daliyeh caves are roughly eight to nine miles north of Old Jericho and seven to eight miles west of the Jordan River. Fifteen hundred feet above the Jordan, or three hundred twenty-five feet above sea level, they can be reached only by foot. Early in January the exploration of the caves began, a dangerous undertaking.[1] Transporting supplies to the explorers was a continual problem. Clouds of dust were stirred up inside the caves when the men entered. Swarms of bats had taken shelter there, and centuries of accumulated droppings produced a hazard to the eyes, lungs and general health of the explorers. In the face of all this, Lapp and his men persisted, and were eventually well rewarded.

Lapp found exciting papyri, business and legal documents of Samaritan origin. With them was a coin, which helped to date the manuscripts at half a century before Alexander the Great (323 B.C.). The period encompassed by the finds ranged from 375 to 335 B.C., the latest of the dates being March 18, 335 B.C. Along with these fragments they dug up pieces of wood, cloth and pottery, as well as the pits of dates and olives.

A startling discovery was of some three hundred skeletons lying scattered about on mats. If these were remains of Samaritans too, what accounted for their presence here, so far away from home? How and why had they died?

[1] "New Light on a Dark Chapter in Jewish History: The Bar Kochba Letters," *Worlds Lost and Found,* Azriel Eisenberg and Dov Peretz Elkins (New York, Abelard-Schuman, 1964).

The Gospel according to Saint Luke, 10:30–37, records this story:

A certain man went down from Jerusalem to Jericho, and fell among thieves, who stripped him of his raiment, and wounded him, and departed, leaving him half dead. And by chance there came a certain priest: and when he saw him, he passed by on the other side. And likewise a Levite came and looked on him, and passed by on the other side. But a certain Samaritan, as he journeyed, came where he was: and when he saw him, he had compassion on him and bound up his wounds, pouring oil and wine, and set him on his own beast, and brought him to an inn, and took care of him. And on the morrow when he departed, he took out two pence, and gave them to the host, and said unto him, Take care of him; and whatsoever thou spendest more, when I come again, I will repay thee.

This story of a generous Samaritan is memorialized in numerous hostels, inns and hospitals — institutions for the care of the sick and of wayfarers. But who were the Samaritans? What was their role in biblical times, and what were their relations with the Jews? The discoveries of the Ta'amireh Bedouins in 1962 have focused new attention on these people, the first sect to have deviated from Judaism — a people who after two millenniums survive today.

High in the hills of Ephraim, in the central district of Palestine, lies Shomrom, or Samaria. Students of the Bible will recall that Omri, king of Israel, founded a capital there in the ninth century B.C. The town gave its name not only to the surrounding area, but also to a small, notable sect, the Samaritans. After the conquest of the Northern kingdom of Israel in 719 B.C. by Assyria, the most warlike nation of its time, the ten tribes of Israel were uprooted and scattered throughout the territory dominated by Assyria. Simultaneously, the Assyrians repopulated the land with tribes and peoples from elsewhere, hoping that by this exchange of populations the original inhabitants would lose their identity and become assimilated in the Assyrian empire.

Sennacherib, ruler of Assyria in the eighth century B.C., recorded the event in an engraving on a monument: "Two thousand, two hundred ninety people I took into captivity; fifty chariots for my military use . . . My captives of war I settled there. . . ."

The biblical narrative of II Kings 17 tells how "the king of Assyria brought men from Babylon and from Cuthah . . . and settled them in the cities of Samaria in place of the children of Israel; and they possessed Samaria and dwelt in the cities thereof." The account goes on to tell how in the early days of their settlement, the new inhabitants "feared not the Lord, therefore the Lord sent lions among them, which slew some of them." Thinking they were being punished because they neglected the god of the land, they implored the king of Assyria to save them by helping them to become acquainted with the god of their new home. So the king ordered one of the priests of Samaria who had been deported to return and "teach them the manner of the God of the land." One of the priests "came and dwelt in Beth-el and taught them how they should fear the Lord." He was evidently an easygoing sort, for in addition to the worship of the God of Israel he allowed each of the peoples that now inhabited Samaria to serve its own god. As this episode is sardonically recorded in the Bible, "They feared the Lord, and served their own gods, after the manner of the nations from among whom they had been carried away." And so, the narrative continues (II Kings 17–34), "do they unto this day."

The period between this event and the return of the Jews to Palestine in 516 B.C. is one of the most obscure in Jewish history, and whatever light can be shed upon it is therefore especially welcome—one more reason why the recent discoveries are so intriguing. The Samaritans reappear at the end of this period as arch opponents to the efforts of the returning Judeans to rebuild the Temple, and indeed as inexorable foes of the Jews. They seem to have usurped for themselves the role of God's chosen people, and proudly called themselves *Shomerim,* from the Hebrew root meaning "observe"—in other words, they prided themselves on their strict observance of the Torah.

Until the discovery of the Samaria papyri, the reconstruction of this period by scholars has been based partly on the biblical narrative and the *Antiquities* of Josephus, and partly on references to the Samaritans in the New Testament and in post-biblical literature. The Samaritans maintain that their history begins with Joshua's conquest of Canaan. They assert that Joshua broke away from Gerizim, the original sanctuary, and established a new holy place at Shiloh. After him came King David, who established the sanctuary at Jerusalem. For the Samaritans, David's temple was known as the House of Shame. They maintained that they were descendants of Ephraim and Manasseh, of the tribe of Jacob, and that their priests traced their ancestry back directly to Eleazar, Phinehas and Aaron, brother of Moses.

The Jews in turn also rejected the Samaritans in the sixth century B.C. This phenomenon is puzzling in the face of biblical evidence that says the Judeans were ready to accept strangers into the fold. We read, for example, in I Kings 8:41–43:

Moreover concerning the stranger that is not of Thy people Israel . . . when he shall come and pray toward this house; hear Thou in heaven Thy dwelling place, and do according to all that the stranger calleth to Thee for. . . .

Much the same attitude is expressed in Isaiah 56:6–7:

Also the aliens, that join themselves to the Lord . . . to love the name of the Lord, to be His servants . . . Even them will I bring to My holy mountain, and make them joyful in My house of prayer . . . for My house shall be called a house of prayer for all peoples.

From these passages, it would appear that non-Judeans were to be accepted providing they practiced circumcision and observed the Sabbath, both mitzvot (commandments of the Torah) followed by the Samaritans. Then why the opposition? The rejection of the Samaritans, it is surmised, may have occurred at a critical historic moment, amid peculiarly dramatic circumstances.

On the twenty-fourth day of Kislev, in 520 B.C., the foundation of the Temple had been laid. According to the account in Ezra 3:10–13, there was song and rejoicing. Learning that the returned exiles were building a sanctuary, certain enemies of Judah and Benjamin (the Samaritans) came to Zerubbabel and the leaders of the people and said they wished to help in the building of the Temple: "For we have sacrificed to the same God as you, ever since Esarhaddon king of Assyria brought us here." But Zerubbabel and their companions answered, "It would not be right for you to build with us, we alone have orders to do so from Cyrus, King of Persia."

Rejected, the Samaritans began to make trouble. They sent a letter denouncing Jerusalem to Artaxerxes, who now ruled in Persia, charging that the Jews planned to rebel once the city had been rebuilt. Chapters 5 and 6 of the Book of Ezra record how the plot of the Samaritans was eventually foiled, in a tale of intrigue and counter-intrigue that ends with the triumph of the Judeans.

However, the Samaritans did succeed temporarily in bringing construction to a halt; and it was not resumed until the second year of the reign of Darius about 523–24 B.C. Then, according to the account in Ezra 5, when the Persian governor, Tattnai, arrived with his retinue to ask on whose authority the reconstruction had been begun, the Jews replied that their authorization had come from Cyrus, in the first year of his reign over Babylon, as they insisted that a search of the Babylonian archives would reveal. The search was duly made, and finally, at the fortress of Ecbatana, a scroll recording the authorization was discovered. Thus the die had been cast; henceforth, for two thousand years the two peoples remained intransigent, each persecuting the other without any move toward reconciliation.

The recent discovery of Samaritan papyri may also serve to clear up one matter that had been a source of contention and puzzlement for many years, among generations of students of Jewish history. The question revolves about the person of Sanballat, an enemy of Nehemiah, Governor of Judea, who is frequently mentioned in the Bible.

When Nehemiah came to Judea from Persia in 445 B.C., Sanballat was governor of Samaria. He plotted against Nehemiah's life, and against the rebuilding of Jerusalem;

but Nehemiah was able to outwit him and to foil his plans. Now it happens that the historian Josephus tells a story of a man named Sanballat who lived in the days of Darius III (335–330 B.C.) and of Alexander the Great. The stories of the two Sanballats both deal with arrangements for a marriage between the ruling family of Samaria and the powerful family of the High Priest at Jerusalem (see Nehemiah 13:28 and Josephus, *Antiquities,* XI, 297–301), and the similarities have confounded the scholars. It seemed incredible that incidents so much alike should be associated with two men named Sanballat who lived many years apart.

The mention of still another Sanballat in the Samaritan papyri now makes it plausible to assume there had been several rulers by the same name. In other words, the governorship was hereditary, the Sanballat of Nehemiah being the first by that name, the one mentioned in the papyrus the second, and the one mentioned by Josephus the third. The evidence in the papyrus may well furnish data on the sequence of governors and thus help in reconstructing Samaria's history and the establishment of the chronology of the period. In addition, the papyri shed light on the social institutions of Persian Palestine and on the development of the language and writing of ancient Hebrew.

The findings from the excavations at Shechem by G. Ernest Wright,[2] begun in 1956, also shed light on the Samaritans. The dig shows that in the third and second centuries B.C., Shechem was settled by Samaritans who had been driven out of Samaria. They even built a temple rivaling the one in Jerusalem. In the years that followed they fortified it. In the war between Darius of Persia and Alexander of Macedonia, it appears that the Samaritans, under Sanballat (the one mentioned by Josephus) sided with Darius.

[2] See *Shechem: The Biography of a Biblical City,* G. Ernest Wright (New York, McGraw-Hill, 1965).

In 331 B.C. Alexander sent an army to punish Samaria. Some of the fugitives who fled to the caves of Wadi el-Daliyeh were suffocated by Alexander's soldiers, who built a fire at the mouth of the cave. This may explain the three hundred skeletons found in the excavations of 1963.

Today there are two groups of Samaritans: one group numbering about one hundred people lives mainly in Holon, south of Tel Aviv; another group of about two hundred forty people lives in Nablus, the site of the ancient Shechem, in the so-called west Jordan area (conquered by Israel after the Six Day War in June 1967), their home for over twenty centuries. The Samaritans of Nablus inhabit the new quarter on the way to the summit of the holy mountain of Gerizim, which is 2848 feet above sea level. It is called by them the Mount of Blessing.

The religious customs of the Samaritans still give clear evidence of their having been a Jewish sect. Their sacred treasure is the Scroll of the Law which they say came down from Abishua, the great-grandson of Aaron, brother of Moses, and which they guard and cherish. Like both Jews and Moslems, they reject any pictorial representation of the Deity. They worship in a synagogue (the Bit Allah, or House of God) which faces toward the Samaritans' holy mountain; the worshippers face Mount Gerizim, not Jerusalem. According to their tradition, the Kohen Gadol, or High Priest, was a direct descendant of Aaron. In 1624 the last Kohen Gadol died without an heir. Since then the appointed religious head has been known as Ha-Kohen or Ha-Levi (of Kohanic or Levite descent). Associated with him is a Shammash (minister) who is alleged to be a descendant of the tribe of Levi. The latter performs the worship service, while the former administers the priestly blessings upon his people.

A Samaritan at prayer

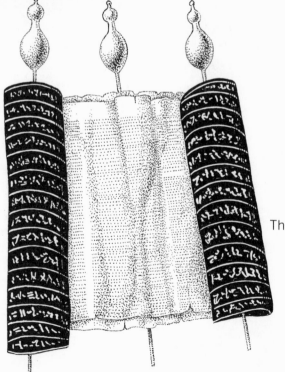

The Scroll of the Law

The Scroll of the Law is written in the Samaritan script, which is older than the present Hebrew writing. Everywhere in the text, the name of Mount Gerizim has been substituted for Mount Moriah or Zion in Jerusalem as found in the Hebrew Bible. In this choice the Samaritans differ not only from the Jews but from Christians and Moslems. The Samaritans revere the Five Books of Moses but reject the Prophets and Writings. These are two of the differences between Judaism and the Samaritan faith.

Intermarriage between Samaritans and Jews is prohibited by both groups although the Samaritans now have all the rights of Israeli citizenship. As a result of isolation and inbreeding, the Samaritans have retained a distinctive physiognomy. The Nablus group speaks Arabic, and every Samaritan has two names, one Arabic and the other Hebraic. They engage mainly in petty trade, and are generally poor and deprived. They have suffered discrimination and extortion at the hands of the Moslems who surrounded them. The rapidly diminishing community might have died out had it not been for the Israeli victory in June 1967, when the two communities of Nablus, on the west bank of Jordan, and Holon, in Israel, were united. Since then, interest in the Samaritan peoples has been rejuvenated and the Samaritan culture has grown.

Recently, a Bible was published in which the pages of the Hebrew and Samaritan texts face each other. A Samaritan printing machine—the only one of its kind in the world—has been created so the group is not dependent upon handwritten manuscripts. As a result, Samaritan horizons are widening, and the outlook for growth of the community is becoming brighter. Hopefully, these ancient people—perhaps the earliest Judaic sect—will regain the prominence which they once enjoyed so long ago.

14

PRICELESS TREASURES UNDER FIRE:
The Dead Sea Scrolls During the Six Day War

On Monday morning, June 5, 1967, Père Roland de Vaux, French Bible scholar and archeologist, was sitting quietly in the library of the École Biblique in the Old City of Jerusalem in Jordan. He was going over plans for the ceremonial reinterment of the founder of the French Bible and Archeology School, which was to take place three days later. The remains of Père Lagrange had been brought there in April from France for reburial in the small plot of ground inside the walled complex of buildings that made up the École Biblique.

Suddenly de Vaux heard a deafening blast, and the table at which he was seated shook violently. A mortar shell from Israeli Jerusalem had fallen just a few feet from the library window. The French savant had barely escaped being wounded or killed.

He ran from room to room through the school warning the other Dominican priests and students. All of them ran quickly into the basement shelter and turned on their radio.

"War has broken out," said the announcer in Arabic. "Fierce fighting is taking place between Egyptians and Israelis in the Sinai desert. This morning King Hussein ordered the Israeli sector of Jerusalem shelled from artillery and mortar positions in the Old City." (Jerusalem had been a divided city since 1948 when, after the State of Israel came into existence, Arab armies attacked Israel and the Jordanians besieged Jerusalem. The Old City of Jerusalem came into Jordanian hands, while the New City became part of Israel.)

Later it became known that Jordanian soldiers had set up two mortar positions right next to the French school. Israeli guns were firing in the direction of the school to wipe out the enemy position, and the École Biblique was in danger of being destroyed. The priests feared for the life of Père de Vaux, one of the most important scholars in the field of the Dead Sea Scrolls. He had been among the original excavators of the Qumran monastery in 1948, and was now editor-in-chief of the project to publish all of the hundreds of scroll fragments from the Judean caves which were in the Palestine Archeological Museum in the Old City.

On Tuesday morning, June 6, Israeli soldiers occupied the building. The soldiers kept the priests and other school residents in the basement shelter until the battle was concluded Wednesday afternoon. After two and a half days of fierce battle, the school emerged relatively unscathed. None of the priests or scholars working there, including Père de Vaux, was injured. The library and other important archeological collections of books and artifacts were unhurt. No bombs had fallen anywhere in the city, and there was no severe damage to the Dominican school complex.

The reburial of Père Lagrange was postponed, of course, but work and studies resumed shortly after the cease-fire on Saturday, June 10. But there was still one central concern in the mind of Père de Vaux after the Six Day War had been concluded: the status of the Dead Sea Scrolls.

One of the key military objectives of the battle for Jerusalem during the Six Day War was the Palestine Archeological Museum (known popularly as the Rockefeller Museum), since it was built like a fortress, having on its tower an eight-sided turret rising over the top of the building. Its strategic location in the Old City, and its fortress-like structure, made it a perfect defense position for the Jordanian army units in Jerusalem. They set up their gun emplacements in its tower and prepared to defend the area from that vantage point.

But what would happen to its priceless archeological treasures, assembled over the past thirty-seven years? This museum was one of the great cultural oases in the Arab countries. Some of the greatest archeological finds from the important excavations of the twentieth century were housed there. What of the Samaria ivories? What about the human skeletons from prebiblical times, some of the earliest in existence? Or the inscription from the Temple of the days of Jesus? Or the famous carved lintel from the door of the Church of the Holy Sepulchre? What would happen to the priceless collection of gold and jewelry from Roman times? Most important of all, would the famous Qumran Scrolls from near the Dead Sea be destroyed after having been preserved for two thousand years?

The Israeli Defense Army had two choices in its attack on the Rockefeller Museum, as it did with all of the cultural and religious holy sites in the Old City. It could bomb and shell these positions and take them within a matter of hours, perhaps even minutes.

Palestine Archeological Museum

Or it could take them through hand-to-hand combat, which would take days of fighting and the loss of many Israeli and Jordanian lives.

To preserve these cultural monuments and the many holy sites sacred to Christians, Moslems and Jews, the Army chose the latter method. After two and a half days of fierce hand-to-hand combat, the Israeli Army captured the Old City of Jerusalem, including the Rockefeller Museum. From the outside, the Museum building showed many signs of the fight. Its walls were pocked with bullets, its windows smashed. Bodies of slain Jordanian soldiers were carried out through its doors. Passersby noticed blood spilled on the stools found in the Qumran monastery on the Dead Sea.

What had happened on the inside? No one knew. Was the damage there as bad as on the outside? Were the priceless treasures smashed, burned or pilfered? Were the Dead Sea Scrolls still there? Were they still preserved in readable condition?

Questions like these filled the minds of the entire community of Jerusalem, as well as of scholars throughout the world. Rumors began to filter out of the country, across the seas to Europe and America during the next few weeks. Israeli authorities would not make any report about the damage sustained until a thorough inventory had been made. Finally an announcement came from the Israeli authorities in Jerusalem. The Rockefeller Museum would be reopened for public visits on July 11, one month after the end of the Six Day War.

Père de Vaux was especially interested in finding out what had happened to the Dead Sea Scrolls. Besides the seven major scrolls, there were hundreds of fragments that had not yet been studied or published.

When July 11 arrived, visitors streamed into the museum. They found that its interior condition was good. Most of the showcases were there. The major difference seemed to be only that the labels on the exhibits and galleries were now in Hebrew as well as in Arabic and English. And the museum now bore a sign out front indicating that it was the property of the State of Israel.

Despite this good news, the special wing which housed the Dead Sea Scrolls was closed. What did this mean? Rumors again began to fly. For two more weeks, the worst was feared.

"The scrolls have been stolen!"

"The scrolls are in Jordan."

"The scrolls are in Israeli Jerusalem."

All kinds of stories and claims were heard. Meanwhile, the truth was that no one in the Old City among the occupying authorities of Israel had any idea what had happened to the scrolls. Israeli scholars believed that when the war broke out, the Jordanians must have whisked the scrolls to Amman, capital of Jordan, on the East Bank of the Jordan River.

One day, a team of Israeli archeologists and soldiers were searching the museum for the scrolls, when a soldier pushed aside one of the display cases. Behind the display case, on the wall, was what looked like a hidden compartment or safe. He quickly called the archeologist in charge of the search.

A team of safecrackers was called in, to make sure that the door of the safe could be removed without causing any damage to the contents. Finally, after laborious and painstaking efforts, the safe door was opened, and the contents emptied out. Inside the safe behind the display case were all seven of the Jordanian Dead Sea Scrolls, plus the four hundred odd fragments!

Soon after, de Vaux was notified, since he was editor-in-chief of the project to publish the scroll fragments. The first question in his mind was: "Who will now have official possession of the scrolls, and the entire museum for that matter?"

A meeting was called by the Israeli Department of Antiquities. The director, Dr. Avraham Biran, was anxious to clarify the status of all the museum property, including the scrolls. At the meeting, Biran explained the situation to Père de Vaux, and other Israeli and overseas archeologists.

"This is the story of recent events," began Biran. "It is well known to you that the history of this great museum goes back to the year 1929, when John D. Rockefeller donated two million dollars for the building, acquisition of the collection and maintenance. In the intervening years, the Palestine Archeological Museum has come into some highly prized collections, most notably the bulk of the Dead Sea Scrolls.

"Up until the year 1948, all of Palestine, including the museum, was governed by the British mandate government created by the League of Nations after World War I. In 1948, the United Nations voted that Jerusalem should become an international city, and that the Rockefeller Museum would henceforth be governed by an International Board of Governors. Jerusalem was never internationalized, as you know, but became split into an Israeli sector (the New City) and a Jordanian sector (the Old City). But the museum has been ruled by the International Board of Governors from 1948 until last year. In November 1966, the Jordanian government nationalized the museum, making it Jordanian government property. Had the Jordanians left the museum under international control, it would remain that way today. But they didn't. And now that Israel has taken the Old City, she becomes the legitimate successor of the former government in such matters. Therefore, the museum is now a part of the State of Israel, as government property, as is the entire city of Jerusalem, old and new."

Père de Vaux felt a bit uneasy about what he was hearing. He was well aware of the fact that the Israelis had just completed a new archeological museum of their own in the New City, the Israel National Museum, and that part of the new museum complex was a special building known as the "Shrine of the Book" which housed the Israeli collection of Dead Sea Scrolls.

Finally, the Dominican Father spoke up. "Do you intend to transfer these scrolls, therefore, to your new museum near the Hebrew University campus, where Professor Yigael Yadin and other scholars are working on their scroll collections? If so, you will be doing a great disservice to me and my colleagues. You know that many of us have been working on this Jordanian collection for years. We are not prepared to have the Department of Antiquities of Israel take over supervision of the publication program after our years of hard work."

"Please, please," said Biran. "You know that we have only the highest regard for you, Père de Vaux, and your associates. You have our guarantee that whatever scholarly endeavors have already been started will in no way be interrupted. You and your associates may continue your research.

"On the other hand, dear friends," spoke Biran as he began to address the others at the meeting, "you know that the group of scholars and archeologists that we have in Israel in the Department of Antiquities and at the Hebrew University's Departments of Bible and Archeology is the largest group of experts assembled anywhere in the world.

"It should be no secret to you," he continued, "that our Israel National Museum is far superior in organization, administration and display techniques to the Rockefeller Museum. Our methods are years ahead of the Palestine Museum. We would never have permitted parts of our collections to be pilfered and sold in the bazaars and antiquities markets in the city, as those in charge of the Rockefeller Museum have. Is it not a fact, also, that the staff of the Rockefeller had not been paid for two months prior to the Israeli takeover on June 7, 1967? This is a reflection of the lack of concern that this museum's former directors and governors have had for their priceless treasures. You can be assured that the archeological collections and displays, including the Dead Sea Scroll collections, will receive the finest attention available anywhere in the world."

"I am greatly relieved," said Père de Vaux. The meeting ended on an amicable and agreeable note, and all were satisfied that the treasures were once again in safe and sound condition. Archeologists around the world were pleased that all of the Dead Sea Scrolls were gathered together under one governing body, the Israel Department of Antiquities, so that all scholars in Israel, Europe and America (the three main centers of biblical and archeological scholarship) could now study the scrolls easily, without having to cross dangerous borders to get to other parts of the collection.

What no one knew at that time was that perhaps the most important of all the Dead Sea Scrolls was yet to be unrolled and read in the days to come, a scroll whose contents had been completely unknown for two thousand years, until it was discovered after the June 1967 War.

15

THE CHOCOLATE-COVERED DEAD SEA SCROLL:
The Story of Yigael Yadin and the Temple Scroll

"All of them are now the property of the Israeli government. Whoever wants to study the Dead Sea Scrolls can study them in one city, without having to cross barbed wire borders between Jordan and Israel."

Speaking at a meeting of archeologists from all over the world, Professor Yigael Yadin of the Hebrew University's Department of Archeology confirmed the report that after the Six Day War all of the scrolls were safe and sound in the hands of Israel's Department of Antiquities. What Yadin did not tell his colleagues was that the newest of all the Dead Sea Scrolls had been recovered only three weeks before and was now in his hands, and that it was the longest and one of the most important of all the scrolls.

During the Six Day War between Israel and Egypt, Jordan and Syria, word reached Yadin (who as a former Chief of Staff received military reports before they were released) that the biblical city of Bethlehem had been captured by Israeli fighters. The archeologist requested army headquarters to search the house of a man named Kando, the Arab antiquities dealer who had negotiated the arrangements for the original Dead Sea Scrolls in 1948.

"On what grounds? What did he do?" asked the officer in charge.

"He has been violating a government law for seven years," answered Yadin. According to a special law of the Kingdom of Jordan, anyone who has possession of a Dead Sea Scroll must offer to sell the scroll to the government through the Palestine Archeological Museum. For seven years Kando neglected to offer the precious scroll to the museum. Now that the museum was in Israeli hands, Yadin was asking the Israeli military government to enforce the Jordanian law, and bring in Mr. Kando.

The action was taken, and the scroll in question was brought to Professor Yadin at the Hebrew University.

When Yadin first gazed upon the scroll, he was very disappointed. He had hoped that it would be in better condition—had Kando delivered the scroll to the Rockefeller Museum when he first received it in 1960 from the Bedouin who found it, it probably would have been. The top of the scroll was in such poor condition that it looked like melted chocolate. While it was in the Dead Sea cave area it had been in a very dry atmosphere, which is ideal for the preservation of parchments. It had probably deteriorated more in Kando's house in Bethlehem during the seven years he had held it, than it did over the whole two millennia. In hilly Bethlehem, the humidity often reaches as high as 70 percent during the winter.

The Temple Scroll

Yadin felt that there was only one man in all of Israel who could unroll this battered scroll without destroying it. His name was David Shenhav, a sculptor who specialized in unrolling ancient parchment manuscripts.

Yadin immediately tried to contact Shenhav. The sculptor, like all Israeli males, had been called up to serve in the army. But two weeks after the war was ended, in late June, Shenhav was able to begin work on unrolling the scroll.

"This is going to be a real tough one," he told Yadin. "We'll have to give it the 'shock treatment.'"

"What do you mean?" asked the archeologist.

"Here is what I propose to do, Professor Yadin. I will first expose the scroll to a very high degree of humidity. At that point I will put it into a freezer for several minutes."

Fortunately, the technique worked, and the scroll began to unroll, and unroll and unroll.

It was extremely long. The two men measured it. It turned out to be twenty-eight feet, three inches, or four feet longer than the longest previously known Qumran scroll, the Isaiah manuscript from Qumran Cave 1.

Upon careful examination, Yadin and Shenhav noticed that a few of the letters were stuck to the back of the sheet against which they had been rolled.

This time it was Yadin who came up with the solution. "I know what we can do," he told Shenhav. "We will photograph the letters as they are, then reverse the negative and we will have straightened out the image."

Finally, the whole scroll was photographed, on prints similar in size to the scroll sheets themselves. Then each print was stapled together in a long roll. Yadin could then roll and unroll it and study it just like the original, without the danger of doing any harm to the real scroll. It turned out that the scroll contained sixty-six columns, with twenty lines each, and that three-fourths of the scroll was in the beautiful handwriting of an ancient scribe.

When the work of unraveling and reading the scroll had finally been achieved, Professor Yadin let his mind run back almost two decades. At that time the first collection of Dead Sea Scrolls was beginning to come to light, in amazingly similar circumstances.

These original scrolls appeared at the beginning of the first Arab-Israeli war, when seven Arab nations attacked the newly born State of Israel. The man who obtained a number of them from Kando in Bethlehem was Yadin's late father, Professor Eleazar Sukenik, also Professor of Archeology at the Hebrew University. (Sukenik's son, Yigael, later changed his name to a Hebraic one, Yadin.)

"I only wish," said Yadin, "that my late beloved father could be alive to share the joy and excitement of knowing that after the Six Day War of June 5–10, 1967, not only have all of the original Dead Sea Scrolls come to rest in Israel, but the newest and longest scroll as well."

In October 1967, Yadin lectured before the twenty-fifth annual meeting of the Israel Exploration Society in the newly reunited holy city of Jerusalem. By that time he had had two months to study the new scroll, now known as the Temple Scroll because of its detailed specifications of the Temple. While he was not ready to publish his full report and translation of the scroll, he made some preliminary ventures as to its background and nature.

To this august international body of scholars, the archeologist reported that the Temple Scroll in many ways was the most significant of all the scrolls.

Like the other Dead Sea documents, the new manuscript had probably come from the Qumran area. It was written by a member of the same monastic sect that had lived at Qumran, and produced such scrolls as "The War Between the Sons of Light and the Sons of Darkness," and "The Manual of Discipline."

These other books are thought by many scholars to have been written by a sect of Jews called the Essenes, who lived during the first century B.C. and the first century A.D. The Essenes were highly disciplined people who decided to leave the active life of the city and reside in the stern, isolated Judean desert. The Qumran sect, whether they were the Essenes or another group like them, had their own calendar. Since the new scroll used the Qumran calendar, it became obvious to Yadin, for that and other reasons, that this Temple Scroll was probably from the same area of the Judean desert, and had been produced by one of the Qumran sect members.

The most unique thing about the documents is that they are meant to be an addition to the Torah (the Five Books of Moses, also known as the Pentateuch). The Temple Scroll was written by a man who believed that God was speaking through him. In the book, God himself speaks, using the first person pronoun, "I." No other Qumran book is written in this way, except for copies of the Bible. While the Temple Scroll was clearly written *after* the other books in the Bible, and as far as we know was never accepted as part of the Bible, it was written with the specific purpose of becoming *part* of the body of literature that was later edited into what we know as the twenty-four books of the Hebrew Bible.

The Temple Scroll is a collection of laws, or a Torah, like the Torah of Moses, from which it quotes. However, the quotes often differ slightly from those in the Bible. Sometimes, entirely new laws are declared, which are found nowhere in the Bible. These new laws probably reflect the needs of the age in which the author lived.

For example, in one law God assigns the death penalty for spying. In the area of ritual purity, an area especially important to the Qumran sect, there are new and even more stringent demands made of the people.

It is a coincidence that this document deals in part with military matters. In one section the scroll talks about how the people of Israel should prepare themselves in case a war of extermination should threaten them — the scroll came to light just as the Arab nations threatened a war of mass extermination, or genocide, against the people of Israel. And, as a direct result of this war, the Temple Scroll was recovered for humanity. Furthermore, although the Israeli nation was not aware of it, they were able to emerge victorious in the June 1967 War because they used the very tactics laid down for such an occasion in the Temple Scroll.

The new scroll declares that if the king of Israel hears of an enemy's threats against Israel, he should mobilize one-tenth of the people. If the enemy is outnumbering and powerful, one-fifth of the people must be called into service. If the enemy begins to advance with a large number of cavalry, one-third of the people should be drafted. Then, when war erupts, one-half of the people are to be conscripted for the battle, while the other half remains at home to defend the homeland.

"This is an excellent description of the various phases of mobilization which preceded the recent Six Day War," says Yadin. "The parallel between the scroll's prescriptions for enlisting the people in time of danger and what actually happened here in Israel two weeks before June 5, 1967, is really fantastic."

Other fascinating items in the Temple Scroll deal with two Jewish holy days never known before. They both follow the biblical festival of Shavuot (Pentecost), which comes fifty days after Passover. A Feast of Oil is celebrated fifty days after Shavuot, and a Feast of Wine fifty days after that. These holidays were based on the calendar used at Qumran and elsewhere at that time, among sects concerned with the end of time, the so-called apocalyptic sects. This calendar was different from the one used by the Jews of Jerusalem, which is still in use among Jews to this day.

Another important difference between the Qumran group and the mainstream Jews of Jerusalem is the very detailed description of the Temple in the new scroll, given for the first time in any Dead Sea Scroll.

The description of the Temple in the new scroll is not similar to the description of the Jerusalem Temple, or to the ones described by the prophet, Ezekiel, or the historian, Josephus. This Temple is obviously the one which was to be built the way the Qumran writer thought it should be.

Yadin points out that the concern about the Temple shows that the Qumran sect was not a Christian-like sect as many scholars had previously thought. The latter would have had no interest in a Temple. The Qumran inhabitants were clearly a Jewish sect with views that differed from the main body of Jewry in Jerusalem in certain important respects.

Thus, almost two decades after the original Dead Sea Scrolls came to light, the Sukenik-Yadin family has shown that the search for, and discovery of, ancient biblical and nonbiblical scrolls in the land of Israel is far from a closed chapter.

Anyone studying about ancient scrolls and archeological finds in today's world must realize that his studies are only as up-to-date as the daily newspaper, when it reports a new discovery. Archeology is a never-ending science. We cannot finish studying about it. We are always in the middle of the book, and the next page may contain tomorrow morning's headlines.

SELECTED BIBLIOGRAPHY

Abramsky, Samuel. *Ancient Towns in Israel.* Jerusalem: World Zionist Organization, 1963

Albright, William F. *From the Stone Age to Christianity.* 2nd ed. Baltimore: Johns Hopkins Press, 1957

Albright, William F. *Archeology and the Religion of Israel.* 5th ed. Baltimore: Johns Hopkins Press, 1956

Baikie, James. *Egyptian Papyri and Papyrus Hunting.* London: Religious Tract Society, 1925

Barton, George. *Archaeology and the Bible.* rev. ed. Philadelphia: American Sunday School Union, 1960

Brion, Marcel. *The World of Archeology.* London: Elek Books, 1962

Burrows, Millar. *The Dead Sea Scrolls.* New York: Viking Press, 1955

Ceram, C. W. *Gods, Graves and Scholars.* rev. ed. New York: Alfred A. Knopf, 1967

Ceram, C. W. *The March of Archeology.* New York: Alfred A. Knopf, 1958

Chiera, Edward. *They Wrote on Clay: The Babylonian Tablets Speak Today.* Edited by George G. Cameron. Chicago: University of Chicago Press, 1938

Daniel, Glyn. *The Origins and Growth of Archeology.* Baltimore: Penguin Books, Pelican Books, 1970

Deuel, Leo, ed. *The Treasures of Time.* New York: World Publishing Co., 1961

Diringer, David. *The Story of the Aleph Bet.* New York: Thomas Yoseloff, 1960

Diringer, David. *The Alphabet.* New York: New York City Philosophical Lib., 1953

Doublhofer, E. *Voices in Stone.* London: Souvenir Press, 1961

Driver, G. R. *Semitic Writing.* London: British Academy, 1954

Eisenberg, Azriel. *Voices from the Past.* New York: Abelard-Schuman, 1959

Eisenberg, Azriel, and Elkins, Dov Peretz. *Worlds Lost and Found.* New York: Abelard-Schuman, 1964

Finegan, Jack. *Light from the Ancient Past.* 2 vols. Princeton, New Jersey: Princeton University Press, 1969

Frankfurt, Henri. *The Birth of Civilization in the Near East.* Garden City, New York: Doubleday, Anchor Books, 1959

Free, Joseph P. *Archeology and Bible History.* Wheaton, Illinois: Kampen Press, 1950

Gelb, Ignace J. *A Study of Writing.* rev. ed. Chicago: Chicago University Press, 1963

Glueck, N. *The River Jordan.* New York: McGraw-Hill, 1968

Goodenough, Edwin. *Jewish Symbols in the Greco-Roman Period.* vol. 9–11, New York: Pantheon Books, 1964

Gordon, Cyrus H. *The World of the Old Testament.* London: Phoenix House, 1958

Gray, John. *Archeology and the Old Testament World.* Camden, New Jersey: Thomas Nelson, 1962

Hawkes, Jacquetta, ed. *The World of the Past.* New York: Alfred A. Knopf, 1963

Kenyon, Frederick. *The Bible and Archeology.* New York: Harper & Row, 1940

Kenyon, Kathleen. *Archeology in the Holy Land.* New York: Praeger, 1970

Kramer, Samuel N. *History Begins at Sumer.* New York: Doubleday, 1959

Kubie, Nora B. *Road to Nineveh: Adventures and Excavations of Sir Austen Henry Layard.* Garden City, New York: Doubleday, 1964

Layard, Austen Henry, ed. by H. W. Saggs, *Nineveh and Its Remains.* (Travelers and Explorers Series) New York: Praeger, 1970

Lloyd, Seton. *Foundations in the Dust.* London: Oxford University Press, 1947

Moscati, Sabatino. *Ancient Semitic Civilizations.* New York: G. P. Putnam's Sons, 1960

Moscati, Sabatino. *The Face of the Ancient Orient.* Chicago: Quadrangle Books, 1960

Orlinsky, Henry M. *Ancient Israel.* Ithaca, New York: Cornell University Press, 1954

de Paor, Liam. *Archeology: An Illustrated Introduction.* Baltimore: Penguin Books, Pelican Books, 1967

Pearlman, Moshe. *Historical Sites in Israel.* New York: Simon and Schuster, 1969

Price, Ira et al. *The Monuments and the Old Testament.* Valley Forge, Pennsylvania: Judson Press, 1958

Pritchard, James B. *Ancient Near East in Pictures,* with supplement. 2nd ed. Princeton, New Jersey: Princeton University Press, 1969

Pritchard, James B. *Ancient Near East*. Princeton, New Jersey: Princeton University Press, 1950

Thomas, Winton. *Documents from Old Testament Times*. Camden, New Jersey: Thomas Nelson, 1958

Thompson, John Arthur. *The Bible and Archeology*. Grand Rapids, Michigan: Wm. B. Eerdmans Publishers, 1962

Wheeler, Mortimer. *Archeology from the Earth*. London: Penguin Books, 1956

Woolley, Leonard. *History Unearthed*. London: Ernest Benn, 1963

Woolley, Leonard. *Digging up the Past*. London: Penguin Books, 1956

Wright, G. E. and Freedman, David N., eds. *The Biblical Archeological Reader*. 3 vols. Garden City, New York: Doubleday, 1962–1970

Wright, G. E. *Biblical Archeology*. Philadelphia: Westminster Press, 1963

Wright, G. E. *An Introduction to Biblical Archeology*. Philadelphia: Westminster Press, 1962

Wright, G. E. *Shechem: The Biography of a Biblical City*. New York: McGraw-Hill, 1965

Yadin, Yigael. *The Message of the Scrolls*. New York: Simon and Schuster, 1957

Yadin, Yigael. *Story of Masada*. New York: Random House, 1969

INDEX

Abner, 46
Abraham, 21
Acropolis, 36
Akkadian, 8, 39, 86
Albright, William Foxwell, 41–6, 48, 86, 87, 91, 94
Amenhotep III, 29
Amon, 26, 30
Amorites, 2
Antiochus VII, 108
Aphrodite, 110
Armstrong, Neil, 18
Ashmolean Museum, 68, 73
Ashurbanipal, 97–8
Assyrians, 14, 20, 44, 60, 65–6, 83, 88, 116–7, 119
Avigad, Nahman, 80, 82–83

Babylon-Babylonia, 2, 3, 8, 9, 11, 12, 13, 60, 84–7, 88, 93, 94–5, 98–100, 102–3, 109, 110, 113, 117, 120
Baghdad, 60
Barton, George A., 52–3, 56
Bedouins, 3, 61, 114, 116, 135
Beirut, 21
Bekah, 57
Bell, Gertrude, 104
Bethlehem, 135, 137
Biran, Dr. Avraham, 131–2
Black Obelisk, 64, 66
Botta, Paul Emile, 60–1

Breasted, James H., 104–5
Byblos, 21

Cairo, 27
Cairo Museum, 33
Canaan (ite), 21, 36, 38, 39
Carchemish, 88
Central Park, 16
Chaldea, 88
Cleopatra's Needle, 16
Constantinople, 61, 98
Cross, Dr. Frank Moore, 114
Cyrus, 95, 97, 100, 102–3, 120

Daliyeh, 115, 122
David, King, 46, 48, 118
Dead Sea, 129
de Morgan Jacques, 2
de Rothschild, James A. (Expedition), 35, 39
Deuteronomy, Book of, 8, 10, 11–3
de Vaux, Pere Roland, 114, 125–6, 129, 131–3
Diringer, Dr. David, 20, 22, 23
Driver, Samuel R., 54
Dura, 105–6, 108, 111–3

Ecbatana, 120
Egypt, 2, 11, 17, 18, 21–2, 26, 32, 33, 71, 88
Egyptian, 16–8, 21, 27, 30, 33, 44
Elam, 4, 8
Elamites, 14
Esagila, 4

Essenes, 139
Esther, 112
Euphrates River, 18, 38, 99
Exodus, Book of, 10–13, 109
Exodus (from Egypt), 32–3, 38–9

Ganneau, Charles Clermont, 75–6, 78–9, 80–3
Garstang, John, 36, 38
Gerizim, 118, 122, 124
Gezer, 53
Gibeah, 42, 44, 46, 48
Goodenough, Dr. Erwin R., 113
Grotius, Hugo, 72

Hamath, 65
Hammurabi, 2–5, 8–14
Hananiah, 93
Haworth, Jeffe, 27
Hazor, 33–6, 38–40
Hebrew, 20–3, 25, 52, 55, 58, 68, 70–1, 74, 76,
    78–9, 81, 84, 124, 130
Hebrew University, 34–5, 56, 80, 132, 134–5
Hezekiah, King, 83
Hittites, 14, 22
Hussein, King, 126
Hyrcanus, 108

Ingholt, Professor Harold, 68, 70–1, 73, 74
Iraq, 14, 63
Isaiah, Book of, 80, 83
Israel (ite), 10–12, 23, 30, 32–3, 35, 39, 44–5,
    46, 54, 57, 93, 95, 103, 116–7, 119, 124,
    126, 130–2, 134, 137–9, 140
Istanbul, 16

Jabin, King of Hazor, 38
Jehoiachin, 87, 89, 91–4
Jehu, King, 65–6
Jerusalem, 34, 39, 41, 43, 48–9, 54, 73, 75, 80–
    1, 83–4, 88–9, 108–10, 118, 120–1, 125–
    7, 131–2, 138, 141
Jimiima, 100
Jordan River, 115, 130

Josephus, Flavius, 109
Joshua, 33, 35, 38, 39, 44, 118

Kassites, 14
Kennard, Martyn, 27
Khorsabad, 60–1
Kish, 4
Koldewey, Robert, 14, 85, 87, 91
Koran, 63
Kurds, 14

Lachish, 33
Lagrange, 125, 127
Lapp, Dr. Paul W., 114–5
Layard, Sir Austin Henry, 61, 63–4, 97–8
Lebanon, 21
Leviticus, Book of, 8, 11, 70
Louvre Museum, 2, 61

Macalister, R. A. S., 53
Marduk, 2, 103
Mari, 3, 4
Meggido, 35–6, 74
Merneptah, King, 28–30, 32–3
Mesopotamia, 8, 18, 20–2, 60, 98, 104
Michmas, Battle of, 54, 57
Mohammed, Abd el Haqq, 42
Mordecai, 112
Mosaic law, 12
Moses, 8, 10, 12, 14, 32, 118
Mosul, 60–1, 63–4, 97
Mount Gilboa, 46
Mount Sinai, 21

Nabataean, 70, 72
Nabonidus, King, 100, 102
Nabopolassar, 85, 88
Naphtali, 38
Nebuchadnezzar, 14, 84–5, 87–9, 91–3
Necho, Pharaoh, 88
Nile, 2, 17, 18, 38
Nimrud, 64

Nineveh, 65, 66
Nuhushta, 89

Omri, 116
Orones River, 65, 66

Pahlavi, 112
Palestine, 11, 12, 15, 32–3, 36, 38–9, 41–2,
    53–4, 66–7, 74–5, 78–9, 86, 116, 118,
    121, 131
Palmyra, 67–8
Persian Gulf, 7, 18
Petrie, Sir Flinders, 26–30, 32
Philistine, 46, 48, 54–5, 56
Phoenicians, 25
Pilate, Pontius, 109
Pilesser III, 14
Place de la Concorde, 16

Qumran, 114, 126, 129, 137, 139, 140–1

Raffaeli, Signor Samuel, 54, 55, 56
Ramses II, Pharaoh, 32
Rashi, 72, 74
Rassam, Hormuzd, 97–100
Rawlinson, Sir Henry Creswicke, 100
Reba, 57
Rich, Claudius James, 60–1
Rockefeller Museum, 127, 129, 131, 133, 135
Rosetta Stone, 18
Rostovtzeff, 105
Ruhi Bey, 43

Samaritans, 115–122, 124
Samuel, Book of, 54–6
Sanballat, 120–1
Sargon, King, 60–1
Saul, King, 42–3, 45–6, 48, 54, 55
Scheil, Father Jean Vincent, 2
Sea of Galilee, 34
Segal, M. H., 56
Seleucids, 105
Sennacherib, 117

Serabit, 21
Shahib, 49, 51–2
Shalish, 57
Shalmaneser III, 65–6
Shamash, 5, 73
Shebna, 80, 82, 83–4
Shechem, 74, 121–2
Shenhau, David, 137
Shomerim, 118
Shomrom, 116
Siloam Tunnel, 82
Silwan, 75, 80, 83
Sinai Peninsula, 21
Solomon, King, 35, 39
Spiegelberg, Dr. Wilhelm, 28–30, 32
Strasbourg, University of, 28
Sukenik, Eleazar, 138, 142
Sumer, 18, 39
Sumerians, 4, 8, 20
Susa, 2, 14
Syria, 3, 15

Talmudic laws, 9
Tell Beit Mirsim, 86
Tel el-ful, 42, 44–5
Tel Hariri, 3
Ten Commandments, 23
Thebes, 26, 28, 33
Tigris River, 18
Titus, 48
Torah, 10

Vincent, Father L. H., 86–7

Weidner, Dr. Ernest F., 87, 91
Wood, Robert, 67–8
Wright, Ernest, 121

Yadin, Yigael, 34–6, 38–9, 82, 132, 134–5, 137–
    9, 141–2

Zedekiah, 89, 92–4
Zerubbabel, 119